MW01714742

From Addiction To Serenity

Vaughn W.

From Addiction To Serenity

by
Vaughn W.

PENTLAND PRESS INC.
ENGLAND • USA • SCOTLAND

PUBLISHED BY PENTLAND PRESS, INC.
5124 Bur Oak Circle, Raleigh, North Carolina 27612
United States of America
919-782-0281

ISBN 1-57197-125-4
Library of Congress Catalog Card Number 98-067420

Copyright© 1998 Terry Wright
All rights reserved, which includes the right to reproduce this book or portions thereof in any form whatsoever except as provided by the U.S. Copyright Law.

Printed in the United States of America

In Memory of Pepper

Thanks

to Bob, who got me started and then kept prodding; to Gary, who always encouraged; to Tom, Dennis, Donnie and Tony for being friends; to Shauncie for her help; and, bless her heart, to Terry, who put up with us all.

Foreword

My name is Bob T., and I am alive today because of the man who wrote this book and his method of working the Twelve Steps of Alcoholics Anonymous. I believe I can speak for hundreds of others who also have had their lives given back to them by their application of the things learned from this gifted and wonderful man.

My encounter with him and his application of the twelve steps happened over eleven years ago. I had tried many other solutions to my problem; none were successful. His simple, straightforward approach penetrated my clouded thinking and sparked something inside me. His ways of working and applying the twelve steps cut through all my bull*#%&.

I was (and still am) an ego maniac with an inferiority complex. I could not admit defeat. Also, I could not get much lower; my abuse of alcohol had destroyed three businesses, my family, and another human life. I had no understanding of self acceptance, ego, humility, powerlessness, unmanageability, pride, or defeat. With the tools the author gave me, I was able to begin to understand these things and much more.

His ways are not easy ways. For me the easy ways just didn't work. I needed "simple." His ways are simple and they do work.

If you've gotten this far, possibly you or someone you love is suffering with an addiction problem. With the help of the appropriate self-help group and this book, one will have the tools necessary to build a whole new life, to encounter happiness and to know serenity. Getting well can and should be an enjoyable experience.

Bob T.

Preface

In no way do I claim credit for the development of the steps discussed in this book. I do claim they helped me find peace of mind. These are the steps born sixty years ago of the desperation of a handful of men and women who found themselves with shattered lives, no hope for the future, and all their plans and dreams trapped in the bottom of an empty whiskey bottle. These are the steps that became the lifeline of a group of people who came to be known as "Alcoholics Anonymous."

The thoughts and ideas about those steps expressed herein are my own opinions, as nearly as possible in my own words. In some cases, I've used a quotation that fits with my opinion and helps me share my feelings about what happiness is and how to achieve it. I concluded long ago that happiness is not something that happens to us; rather, it is something we do. Abraham Lincoln said, "Most people are about as happy as they make up their minds to be." Someone (I don't remember who) said, "People are happy when they are not acutely aware of being miserable."

I was always "going to be happy." I was going to be happy when I got out of school; I was going to be happy when I got out of the army; I was going to be happy when I got a better job; always over the next hill or around the next corner or after the next sunrise, I was "going to be happy." I never seemed to find, in any of the things I did or in any of the places I happened to be, that elusive euphoria that I thought happiness must be.

When I finally realized I needed to get out of myself to be happy, I didn't know how to do that because I didn't know myself. I had tried to use the steps discussed in this book, but only in a superficial way—because that was the way I did most everything. The result was disappointment. Finally, though, when almost everything was gone and I had made a shambles not only of my life, but also the lives of some others, I examined the steps word for word. And understanding set in like cement.

It is my prayer that this book will help someone, somewhere, avoid the pitfalls and dead ends I ran into in my own search for happiness, serenity, and peace of mind.

There are a number of self-help groups who use the Twelve Steps as a method of recovery and maintenance—Alcoholics Anonymous (the group who introduced the steps), Overeaters Anonymous, Narcotics Anonymous, and Sex Offenders Anonymous, for example. There are far too many people who try these groups for a time but give up, believing that it does not help. Maybe it is because these unfortunate individuals do not understand how to use the steps.

This book is not intended to replace anything ever written about overcoming addictions. Rather, it is a book of methods. My methods. It is safe to say I have shared these methods with hundreds of people and have seen them work time and time again for those who were facing defeat—but faced it and won.

Every one of us, from the richest to the poorest, strongest to the weakest, is powerless over something. Some problem in our lives either has defeated us or will. Recognition and acceptance of this fact is the first step to coming out on top of the many problems we will all face in life. Sometimes we "gotta lose to win." Sometimes we need someone to help us.

But for whatever reason, our egos seem to drive us to go it alone, to suffer in silence and eventually succumb to our worst enemy, whatever we conceive that to be. Actually our worst enemy is that very ego that refuses to admit defeat—in other words, our pride.

Senator Allan Simpson of Wyoming once said to me, "If self acceptance isn't the name of the game (of life), then I'm in the wrong ball park." Absolutely. Self acceptance, but not pride. (Self acceptance will help us understand our limitations, recognize our strengths, and use both as tools for accomplishment.)

I read that Henry Ford's success was due to the fact that he used this very principle to gather around him a team of people that could do what he knew he could not, and that could and would support him in the things he could do.

Some people seem born understanding the importance of the difference between self acceptance and pride, while others learn it early, others have to be taught, and still others go through life never knowing.

What I have attempted to do in this book is to share what I know to be a method for developing the self-esteem that leads to happiness and serenity. Far be it from me to say other methods don't work, but I know for sure that what does not work is using no method at all.

Do not expect my methods to "make you well" overnight. If you are in a predicament, it probably took a long time to develop, and the problems will take some time to unravel. Do not expect my methods to be easy; neither expect them to be too hard. In the meantime, associate yourself with the appropriate self-help group, remembering that no one need know, because "Anonymous" means just that. Anonymous.

Have fun getting well.

Addiction

According to the New Lexicon Webster's Dictionary, addiction is: n. the state of being addicted. I didn't find this to be very helpful. However, if we check out addict, the book has this to say: n. a person addicted to something harmful, usually a drug; (loosely) someone inordinately fond of something not harmful. Not harmful? Too much of just about anything can be harmful, to my way of thinking, and to my way of thinking, addiction will lead to too much. So I also thought this was not very helpful.

Food, normally not harmful, can become extremely hazardous when someone is addicted to eating, hence "Overeaters Anonymous." And if we think about it, humans can become addicted to almost anything, therefore making almost anything hazardous. You can be addicted to work, sex, money, tobacco, gambling, speeding, stealing (which would be harmful in any case), reading, sleeping, drugs, alcohol, eating, and even walking. I once knew a man who was addicted to walking. Every day he could be seen walking the streets of the town he lived in, and he wasn't just strolling along, he was walking as if he had somewhere to go in a hurry. But he had nowhere to go, and when someone finally realized he had a problem, he was sent away for help. When he returned home, he was as normal as you or me.

My own definition of addiction would contain the words "mental compulsion," because addicted people seem compelled to engage in their own self destruction. They don't realize that self-destruction could be the end result of their compulsive behavior.

Addicted people seem to be operating under a mental compulsion, real enough, coupled with a physical need, real or imagined, to engage in what anyone would consider abnormal activities. I believe the cause is an inordinate need to feel better than they normally do. I knew a lady who was addicted to shopping. She went shopping every day and often did not buy anything because she didn't need anything other than to go shopping. Her husband was a heavy drinker, drinking every day to the point of intoxication;

she went shopping as a means of escape. When her husband overcame his drinking problem, she overcame her shopping problem.

I believe that people who become addicted to alcohol, as I did, for example, do so as a result of a desire to feel better—to alleviate feelings of inferiority, alienation, rejection, rebellion, anger, fear, resentment and other strong negative feelings about themselves and the world around them. They seem to feel they have been left out, passed over, ignored and rejected by the human race, and they seek a means of escape from such feelings.

They see themselves as unimportant, unwanted, unloved, unneeded, and any other "uns" they can conjure up and use as an excuse for overindulgence in anything that gives them temporary relief.

All these "un"-happy feelings are covered up with bravado, acting out, attention seeking, and unsavory behavior of various kinds, as they try to impress, stand out, and be recognized as important by someone, anyone, somewhere, anywhere. Later they view all this with regret, even shame, and then they repeat it again and again until something drastic comes along to interrupt the cycle. Sometimes it is recovery. Sometimes it is insanity. Sometimes it is death.

To my knowledge, there is no known cure for addiction. I don't mean to imply that the gentleman can never go for a walk again without taking off uncontrollably. Neither do I mean the lady can never go shopping again. What I do believe, though, is that the lady's husband can never again drink with impunity because his particular kind of addiction can be arrested, but never cured. Neither can a person addicted to harder drugs ever again use those drugs without losing control and going off the deep end or over the curb. There are "kinds" of addictions. Once the gambler gains control of his problem, he cannot gamble again without losing the family jewels, assuming there are any left. The over-eater, once in control of the problem, must not take chances with his recovery, but obviously that is not to say food is totally off limits now and forevermore!

If addiction has underlying causes, I think the underlying causes have underlying causes. Let's take a look at how the seeds of addiction might be planted, and how they can grow and eventually blossom into a bouquet of destructive feelings, thinking, and behavior.

People have a tendency to ask little children what they want to be when they grow up.

At least it was so when I was little. I lived next door to a man who played the drum in our local drum and bugle corps. Now there was a sharp outfit. They wore shiny, silver helmets shaped like those worn by American troops in the first World War. They wore white shirts, red ties, and white pants with a bright red stripe down the outside of the leg, and a bright red sash around their waists, and shiny black knee-high boots. The music they played was absolutely thrilling to a four-year-old kid.

At the same time I lived but a block from a branch of the Burlington Northern Railroad where twice a day the "motor" went by; that was another thrill, but not quite as thrilling as the Union Pacific locomotives that roared past just a few blocks up the street from my home.

And the fire trucks! Remember the excitement they caused any time you saw them racing past on their way to what we didn't know was a very dangerous, frightening job? Huge shiny red-and-chrome trucks streaking past at probably 25 miles an hour, sirens screaming, with the men hanging on the sides and back wearing their exceptionally fascinating helmets and knee-high rubber boots. What a sight to see when I was a little kid!

So it was natural, I think, when someone asked me what I wanted to be when I grew up that I would answer drummer, railroad engineer, or fireman, depending upon which I had most recently seen.

I do not remember ever telling anyone that I wanted to grow up to be a drunk. For one thing, I had no role model for that occupation, or more accurately, "un"-occupation. My father, my grandfathers, my uncles, and, as far as I know, my neighbors were all sober people. Not to say they never drank, but they hadn't been drinking long, because prohibition wasn't repealed until I was four years old, and if the stuff was around I don't remember seeing any evidence of it. So I don't remember ever saying I wanted to grow up and be a drunk. But I did become a drunk. Later on we'll discuss whether I ever grew up.

I'm sorry to say I learned to dislike school when I was in the fourth grade. That is when I learned that school teachers can be thoughtless and unjust. It would be pointless to go into the details of that, but I think it is worth saying the problem was compounded by the woman who "taught" me in the sixth grade. I believe that is when the feelings of inferiority began to dominate me. I was from a poor family and I badly needed new shoes. My father couldn't do a thing about it, so he had me wear a pair of my sister's shoes to school.

YOU HAD TO THINK & COM TO A DECISON BASED ON YOUR THINKING NO FEELING

I felt very self-conscious that day. The shoes were white with a moderate heel. Knowing full well I was going to be teased by other kids, I clowned around a bit when I came into the room. The teacher took immediate exception to that, called me a show-off and told me I had better not come back to school after lunch with those shoes on my feet. Naturally the other students thought this was very funny. The only choice I had was to wear the shoes after lunch or go to school barefooted. That day I learned to hate school teachers. My dislike for school also became hatred.

My family moved a lot as my dad sought work, and when I entered the eighth grade I was entering my seventh school building. I guess I was thirteen years old then; I had a full-blown resentment towards a lot of things and a fully-developed sense of being inferior, a feeling that I really did not belong in this world. Imagine changing schools in mid-term and finding that while you had been learning general math, your new classmates were half-way through the study of fractions; where you had been learning all about the Plains Indians, your new classmates were learning about Eohippus. That is one way to begin feeling out of place.

At this point, we all should be saying, "Awww! Poor baby." Exactly. That is the way I was feeling—poor pitiful me, ain't it awful! Nobody loves me, everybody hates me, guess I'll go eat worms. Self pity, anger, resentment, envy, fear and all kinds of negative junk. I didn't know what the hell to do about it. But it was also at that age I found the magic elixir!

I had chosen my friends from a school on the other side of town. We would meet at the bowling alley; in fact, at one time or another we all worked there as pin setters. So one chilly night we met and I was greeted with the news that one of my pals knew where an unlocked beer truck was parked. I had become a sort of combination Huckleberry Finn and Jesse James, and if I shouldn't, I would. So we did. We each stole a quart of beer and a couple of blocks away, behind a billboard at a closed gas station on this chilly night, we drank it. I wasn't thirsty. I didn't like it. I drank it only because they were going to, and they drank it only because I was going to. It was a kind of "I dare ya" situation.

My whole world changed then. Everything in the world was rosy and warm. I felt strong, I felt handsome, I felt witty, and above all, I felt, for the first time in years, if ever, that I was okay. I recognized right away where those feelings came from. I wanted to go back and steal another quart of beer and said so. The other guys said they'd rather do something else.

Guess what? I was hooked. I was, right then and there, psychologically addicted to the feelings that alcohol produced within me. My body was not hooked; that doesn't happen with alcohol until it has been abused for a few years, but I suppose that differs with each person. My mind was addicted. I have never forgotten that first experience with alcohol. One of those same pals, a few years later, gave me a small plaque with this message inscribed on it:

> "When your heels hit hard, and your head feels queer,
> and your thoughts foam up like the froth on beer,
> and your legs are weak, and your voice is strong,
> and you laugh like hell at some damn fool song
> —you're drunk, by gosh, you're drunk."
>
> –Anonymous

What a strange thing for a young boy to keep on his bedroom wall when others his age are hanging posters of baseball players. But I thought it was great, and it perfectly described the feelings I would get when I got (or made) the opportunity to drink. I looked forward to every chance to "get a buzz on."

That is one of the earliest symptoms of alcoholism. Dr. E. M. Jelinek, an early pioneer in the study of alcoholics and alcoholism, refers to this as "preoccupation with alcohol." I was definitely preoccupied with drinking by the time I was in high school. It was no longer beer that I was interested in, but whiskey. I would plan ways to get it and look forward to Friday nights, when I could always find some "kindly inebriate" who would buy a pint of whiskey for me. Friday nights—when other kids were at a football or basketball game or school dance or some other normal activity, I would be drinking. Saturday nights were soon added to the schedule, and in the summer time, some weeknights as well.

I'm sure plenty of other kids had the negative attitudes and feelings I had developed and had found more appropriate ways to deal with them. But I had met Ethyl Alcohol, and she and I were having a love affair that increased in intensity and frequency of visits with each passing year.

Another early symptom of alcoholism, according to the same study, is labeled "increased tolerance," meaning the "victim" soon develops a need to use greater quantities of the drug to gain the same effect that was experienced in the beginning. It isn't long before the person becomes known as one who can "hold their liquor." When this happened to me I considered it an accomplishment. I had no idea at the time how scary this condition is.

I was not a daily drinker, but each time I drank, I did so to excess. The use of alcoholic beverages costs money, and the more you drink the more you spend. Usually I was spending money I could not afford to spend. This, too, is an early symptom of alcoholism. It has been named "extravagance." The spending of too much money led to feelings of "guilt and remorse," another symptom of the disease. This just doesn't happen to normal people, or if it does, they make damn certain it does not happen again. Alcoholics do it over and over again, each time swearing it will not re-occur, but in time giving in once more to that impulse that leads to a drunk. When asked why it happened again, they do not know but will give all sorts of reasons, ranging from various conditions of the weather to various attitudes toward some person, place or thing. Always, they seem able to verbally justify what happened. This is yet another symptom—"rationalizing and externalizing to justify another episode of drinking." "My team won, my team lost, the weather was hot, cold, rainy, or dry, and besides, if you had a mother-in-law like mine, you'd drink too." When they are not believed, they may become indignant and use the nonbelief as an "excuse" to turn right around and do it again—still another symptom.

It is never the alcohol that is a problem with the addicted drinker. I remember a night long ago when I was given a quart of apricot brandy. I drank it all that evening and was I sick. I continued to drink for another eighteen years, but for fifteen of those years I would not eat apricots. This is, of course, ridiculous—but not to a drug-affected mind that becomes threatened to the point of total denial by the idea of giving up the drug. Ethyl alcohol and other mind- and mood-altering drugs do not produce rational thinking. "Inappropriate thinking" is another symptom studied by Doctor Jelinek. A drug-affected brain cannot think rationally, even though it thinks it is doing so. Consequently, drug abusers are very often obnoxious, boisterous, combative, and generally objectionable.

The story is told of three men in the waiting room of a psychiatrist's office. One had been diagnosed manic depressive, one was a pseudo neurotic, and one was an alcoholic. After waiting a considerable time, one of the men decided to get acquainted with the others. Extending his hand to the man next to him, he said, "As long we have to wait here together, we may as well get acquainted, don't you think? My name is Napoleon." The other man gave him a hostile look and said, "You're not Napoleon, I am." "Oh, sir, you're mistaken, for I am Napoleon." "Oh, no you're not, I am." This went back and forth for a little bit of time and finally the first man demanded, "Who told you that you are Napoleon?" The other responded, “God did.” Whereupon the alcoholic jumped to his feet and exclaimed, “I did not!” Delusions of grandeur—another symptom.

Aggressive, abusive behavior is a symptom I look back on with deep regret. Many things I did would never be done by a person not under the influence of a drug. It is when I think of those things that I truly want to reach out and help someone find a way out of such a messy life. I know of three times I struck my wife. Many more times she was verbally abused and I now believe she was emotionally abused every day of our married life. Did I think I was God? I don’t honestly know what I thought, but I do know that the God I believe in never gave me permission to abuse another living being, and certainly not my wife.

Under the influence of the drug, whether I was using at the time or not, I became a liar, a cheater, a thief, a bum. I had stopped long ago getting that good feeling of relief I first experienced from using alcohol. What I got instead was shame, remorse, fear, and physical and mental illness. But I could not resist the compulsion to drink. From the age of thirteen this problem plagued me, accelerating as the years went by until, as William Shakespeare so aptly put it, it made me “frankly despise myself.” Only by the grace of the God I believe in was I released after twenty-five years. After that, I was able to go about the business of helping others. You can read about this in my version of Steps One and Twelve.

YOU WERE ALL THAT BEFORE YOU EVER took A DRINK - YOU WERE BORN A SINNER IN ALL THOSE WAYS + OTHER. PROBLEM IS NOT ALCHOL BUT SELF, EGO, WANTING TO BE IN CONTROL "GOD"

THINK OF OUR THINKING BEFOR A RELAPES

Step One

WE ADMITTED WE WERE POWERLESS OVER ALCOHOL, THAT OUR LIVES HAD BECOME UNMANAGEABLE

It was early in November
As near as I remember,
While walking down the street in tipsy pride,
No one was I disturbing
As I lay down at the curbing
When a pig walked up and lay down by my side.
As I lay there in the gutter
Thinking thoughts I dare not utter,
A lady passing by was heard to say,
"You can tell a man who boozes
By the company he chooses."
And the pig got up and slowly walked away.

—Author Unknown

Shortly before the end of my twenty-five year drinking career, I had a particularly debilitating hangover one morning, and the girl who had put up with my insanity for many, many years was no longer willing to put up with it. Sick beyond any possibility of working, even if I could have gotten out of bed, cleaned myself up, and managed to get to the job, I asked her to call my boss to tell him I was sick and wouldn't be in that day. Her response was simple, brief and, I knew even in my haze, final. "Do it yourself." Consequently, I did not go to work that day and my boss was not notified.

Later in the afternoon, when I was able to get up, stand up, and clean up, I called my boss and asked if he would meet me at a coffee shop when he got off work. He was one of those men who seem to be born with tolerance and patience as outstanding characteristics, and he agreed to meet with me.

Allow me to give you a bit of background. I had, prior to this time, found my way to Alcoholics Anonymous and had been in treatment for alcoholism three different times for a total of one hundred and eighty-five days. In one of the treatment situations, I had been what I considered brutally honest with myself, and, as a result, remained dry for approximately ninety days. In other words, I failed. But I had learned something of the basic philosophy of the AA program of recovery and something of myself as well. I knew that honesty was an absolute must for continued sobriety, even though at that point I had no understanding of what sobriety really is.

I could no longer find a job in the area where I lived, so had found a new job in a new location where I was not known. During the interview for that job, my prospective employer asked me, among other questions, whether I had any problem with alcohol. There is an old joke about that. According to the joke, the answer to the question is, "No, I only have a problem finding enough of it." But my answer, because I had been dry something like ten weeks, was simply, "No."

Because of missing work that day, I now had to face my boss, after working for him approximately two months with that lie in the background. We met at the small coffee shop and sat across the table from each other, face to face. "The reason I was not at work today," I began, "was because I was sick. The reason I was sick is that I had a terrible hangover from drinking last night." Then, after two years at AA and one hundred eighty-five days in treatment, for the first time ever totally believing it was true, I said, "The reason I drank last night is that I am an alcoholic."

Obviously my boss had every reason to can me on the spot, and I'm certain some would have done so. He didn't. Instead he told me he had some past experience with alcoholics, that he respected me for coming to him in this way, and that he was willing to work along with my problem if I was willing to try to overcome it. Of course, I assured him I was, which does not mean that was an end to my drinking. The end came on the following September thirtieth, perhaps a month later.

I firmly believe, and in fact, I insist, that Step One is not something I did, but is something that happened to me as a result of all I had done, or not done, due to my frequent and sometimes constant drinking, my selfishness, my arrogance, my lying, cheating, stealing, brutality and all the other forms the disease takes.

It came on a warm, clear Sunday afternoon and ended after midnight. My wife sent me on some small errand to the drug store. After making whatever the purchase was, I stepped out into the beautiful day and ruined it. I ruined it for her, for my fifteen-year-old-son, for myself and perhaps for some other people that I don't even know about. I decided to have just one drink. For the alcoholic, that is a lie right out of the mouth of hell. No alcoholic ever wants one drink, but all practicing alcoholics can convince themselves, in the blink of an eye, that they do want just one, and that this time, having failed a thousand-thousand times before, they can and will have just one. My follow-up thinking ran thus: I will drive to a bar that I know of in the country, have one drink of vodka, eat a breath mint, eat two breath mints, eat a whole package of breath mints, drive home, spend the day with my family, and no one will be the wiser.

By the time I reached the bar, I had decided that since I was going to drink vodka, which I believed was much less noticeable on the breath, and eat all those breath mints for added insurance, that I may as well order a double, which I did.

After that drink, I was deciding whether one more might not be appropriate when a man and woman wearing cowboy hats came and sat at the bar next to me. They looked like very friendly people (whom, incidentally, I don't recall ever seeing again after that day) and since I'm a man who likes to make friends, it seemed only right that I offer to buy them a drink. Knowing that most people with common sense do not like to drink alone (I had done it a hundred times or more), I decided that I should also have another and then excuse myself to go home to my family. This being done, the nice couple wanted to reciprocate. One does not want to seem impolite to new friends, so of course I accepted and they did and I did and they did and I did. . . .

Most of the rest of that day is blacked out from my memory, but what I share with you now I will never forget. It was just about midnight when the bartender, another new friend I had made that day, spoke to me saying, "Hey, you." He demonstrated the rest of what he had to say by pointing, first at me, then at the door. I took that to mean he would be pleased to see me leave the premises. I do not know what obnoxious thing I had said or done nor to whom I had done it. But past experience with bartenders who outweigh me by seventy pounds or so coupled with his facial expression made me think it might behoove me to exit, which I did.

The thing to do following an experience of this kind is to become angry and add shame to shame, the better to amplify the guilt that one can enjoy later on. So I became angry. Driving home I began to build up the defense. Everyone knows, but no one knows better than the alcoholic, that the best defense is a good offense. So when I arrived home, my wife had become the villain.

> It hath pleased the devil drunkenness to give place to the devil wrath. One imperfection shows me another to make me frankly despise myself. To be at once a man, by and by a fool and presently a beast. Each inordinate

> cup is unblessed and the ingredient is a devil. Oh, thou invisible spirit of wine, if thou hast no name to be called by, let us call thee devil.
>
> –William Shakespeare

So the young man who told her he loved her, cherished her, wanted her to marry him and allow him to ever care for her, came home to his wife after midnight that night and heaped verbal abuse upon her that no human being should ever endure. I don't know what I said. I do know I was loud and profane and that I kept it up for a long time. I am surprised that some well-meaning neighbor did not call the police.

Things were about to change. Consider the civil war. General Lee found himself in no position to continue fighting. He recognized that he was defeated. This great man did not want to surrender, far from it. He wanted to win. He wanted to keep fighting and to achieve victory. But he realized he and his army would be destroyed if he chose any route but surrender. Defeat stared him in the face, a painful experience for anyone.

As I write, I have only to raise my eyes to a picture of my son, a man of whom I am extremely proud and for whose courage as a fifteen-year-old boy I am eternally grateful. Even as I write, the tears come with the remembrance of the climax of my drinking career. These are not tears of sadness, self-pity or any of that garbage, but these are tears of gratitude. That son was in his room that night, needing to sleep because he would have school in the morning. He was listening to a drunken tirade again.

He came from his room and stepped in front of me, his feet spaced wide apart, his fists doubled and held close to his chest. His blue eyes were staring straight into mine. His teeth were clenched and he spoke between them, "Knock it off, Dad, I'm not gonna take it anymore." Ten words. It was as if he held a mirror up in front of my face, for I saw myself then as I had never seen myself before—a drunken sot, a nothing, a gob of spit. I remember wishing I could vomit myself into the rug and disappear, because like I have never hated anything or anyone before or since, I hated the man I saw and recognized as myself.

At the same time, a new feeling came over me, a feeling of release. I was free. I never had to take another drink. It was as though God Himself had reached down, put His hand on my shoulder, and said, "That's enough." And it was enough. I still do not have to take a drink. I am still free. That is not a guarantee or a promise that I will not take a drink, only that I do not have to.

That is the Step One experience. When I recognized defeat, when I stopped fighting and was willing to surrender, when I just gave up, my obsession to drink was gone. It has not returned. I began my victory over alcoholism not out of strength, not out of power of the will (because willpower works on alcoholism the same way it does on diarrhea—in other words, not at all), but by my finally admitting defeat and surrendering. It was simply a matter of, "I can't do it, God can; I think I'll let Him."

A few years later, as reported to me by someone else, my son was sharing the story of a drunk and his family with a group of people, whether a church group or a school group I don't know. When he finished, he told them, "The man I have told you about was my father. After that, we grew up together." My opinion: he grew up and I'm still working on it. At any rate, we became, and are to this day, very good friends.

Now that I have shared my Step One "experience" with you, let's think about Step One as it is written.

We admitted we were powerless over alcohol—that our lives had become unmanageable.

As a child, I had no ambition to grow up and be a drunk, and I have never met anyone who did. That would be preposterous to the extreme. I wanted to be a fireman, a railroad engineer, an airplane pilot and a drummer in the local drum-and-bugle corps, just like any other little boy wants. By this, I know that alcoholism is not something I did, it is something that happened to me. It is not a moral issue; it is a disease. Self-induced, say some. But if so, I'm sure it's unintentional. No one wants to be a drunk.

I have no power over alcohol. If anyone does, it is political power, for I have no say as to how much is brewed or distilled, where it is brewed or distilled, where it is sold or by whom, what price is charged for it, who may buy it or who may drink it or how much they can drink. If I drink it myself, I have no idea how much I will drink or when I will stop. I am powerless over the stuff.

So let's look at what I think the second half of the step means, "our lives had become unmanageable." My early attempts to use this program as a road to happiness, serenity, and peace of mind were feeble, therefore fruitless. I committed the steps to memory. That just gave me a mouthful of words that might have impressed someone else for a while but brought about no change in my attitudes, therefore no change to speak of in my behavior. I simply didn't understand.

That I could not manage my life meant to me that I could not manage the daily affairs of living, such as how to make a lot of money, how to get what I wanted when I wanted it, and how to get people to get along with me by doing things the way I knew they should be done. It took the naked truth, reflected in the eyes of my son, to awaken me to the need to think.

Unmanageable is not the key word here. What is unmanageable is the important thing to consider, and the step says "life" is unmanageable. Oh, then that explains it, right? No, it does not, or at least it certainly didn't for me. The question finally occurred, and I think the angels must have cheered, "WHAT IS LIFE?" Over the years I have asked that question of a lot of people and the answers were almost, not quite, standard. "Well, it's living," they would say, or they might interchange the word "existing" for living, or someone might tell me that life is "doing things." Mostly when I asked the question, the response I received was a sort of embarrassed shifting of position, a loss of eye contact, a small, self-conscious smile, a discreet cough behind the hand and finally the admission, "I've never really thought about it."

Isn't that amazing? Isn't it sad? Here we are, talking about the most precious commodity in the world, something that almost no one would knowingly exchange for any price, and when asked to define it, we "haven't really thought about it." I, too, was guilty for much too long of not taking time out to examine it, to "think about it." The beloved Charlie Brown would say, "Good grief!" But after memorizing the steps, I could glibly recite "our lives had become unmanageable." Since I had no idea what I was talking about, it was not a very long period of time before I was drunk again and bewildered as to why. By the grace of God and the courage of a fifteen-year-old boy, I was brought face to face with a need to think.

At times when talking about life with people, I have tried a little experiment in order to make the point that I think is necessary in order to use Step One to advantage. So let's try it here. Let's imagine there is a body on a table in front of us. A dead body. We will use a rabbit if you are squeamish about dead human bodies. Let's take a pin and poke the body. What happens? Nothing. Why? Because it is dead. Let's imagine again, this time a live body. When we poke it with our pin, what happens? Protest in some form. If it happens to be a human body, it is apt to put out our lights. Why? Because it is alive.

So what is the difference? The live body FEELS. The dead body does not. Where there is life, there is feeling. Where there is no life, there is no feeling. We are constantly feeling. If we love, that is a feeling. If we hate, that is a feeling. Fear is a feeling, hunger is a feeling, sleepiness is a feeling. You can feel yourself on the seat of your pants when you're sitting, the bottoms of your feet when you're walking, and so on.

The conclusion is obvious: since there is apparently no feeling in death and there are endless feelings in life, life and feelings are one. LIFE IS FEELINGS. THERE IS NO DEATH ETURNAT LIFE

Look at the step again. We admitted we were powerless over alcohol, that our FEELINGS had become unmanageable. When this finally soaked in, I found it much easier to understand the step as well as myself. I was no longer so mystified by behaviors from the past that had devastated my self-esteem. I was able to recognize the almost manic depressive episodes of my life and to understand the cause of almost all of them. It became clear to me that I was too happy, too sad, too selfish, too generous, that I loved too much, hated too much, and in general, popped up and down emotionally like a yo-yo. I had been on a runaway roller coaster ride, unpredictable to myself, let alone others. I thought I was finding relief in alcohol and you know what? That ain't normal.

STEP ONE FROM WHAT?

We admitted we were powerless over WHATEVER our problem is, that our FEELINGS had become unmanageable.

Step One is not something you do, it is something that happens to you—such as the confrontation by my son.

NOTES

OUR DESIRES, EGO, PRIDE, SELF SATISFACTION, SELF WILL ECT UNMANIGABLE

Step Two

CAME TO BELIEVE THAT A POWER GREATER THAN OURSELVES COULD RESTORE US TO SANITY

A guy got drunk at a company picnic and was wandering around at the edge of a cliff when he tripped on a tree root and fell over the edge. Part of the way down, a small tree was growing out of the side of the cliff, and he was lucky enough to catch hold of it. So there he hung, suspended a couple hundred feet from the bottom. He began to sweat.

Shortly, he heard a voice call his name: “Sam.” He looked up, down, and all around, but saw no one. Again he heard the voice: “Sam.” Looking around, he still saw no one and he decided it must be God calling him. “Yes, Lord?”

“Sam, do you believe in me?”

“Yes, Lord, I sure do.”

“Do you believe I put that tree there so you could grab hold of it?”

“Yes, Lord, I sure do believe that!”

“Well, Sam, do you believe I can lift you back up to the top of the cliff?”

“Oh, yes, Lord, I sure do believe.”

“Well then, Sam, let go of the tree.”

“Like HELL I will! D’ya think I’m crazy?”

What does it take in an individual life before we really believe we need help? We can express belief, but what does it take before we feel belief? What does it take in an individual life before we are willing to accept help at any level? From any source? I get the sense that our friend Sam waited too long.

Step Two addresses, along with our obsession to drink, the inability to manage our feelings: inappropriate sadness, anger, selfishness, self-pity, greed, lust, pride, and all the other character defects that we will examine closely in Step Four.

"Unmanageable" (as used in Step One) implies the uncontrollable. Uncontrollable feelings, whether under the influence of alcohol or not, cause abnormal behavior, and abnormal behavior can be easily defined to mean insanity.

When I first read this step I saw, as I believe many people do, ". . . came to believe IN a power greater than ourselves . . ." rather than THAT a power greater than ourselves could restore us to sanity.

If there is a key word to better understanding of this step, it is the word THAT. "Came to believe THAT a Power greater than ourselves could do something about our problem." With the guidance of these steps, all of them, and the help of other people who have already experienced them, that Power can bring about a significant personality change—significant enough to allow us to overcome traits that have become so ingrained that we fail to recognize them, much less know how to manage them.

Most of us fear change because we expect it to bring about something unknown, something that we believe we may not be able to adjust to. Therefore, we are apt to resist it with all our might until we understand it. Result? Denial, excuses, projection. "If you had a mother-in-law like mine . . . " and so forth, to our own hurt.

But consider this: insanity is not apt to get better by itself, it is apt to get worse. It just very possibly, with continued use of alcohol and other mind-altering drugs, will come to an irreversible, horrifying end.

When I first approached this step, I assumed that the use of the word "sanity" referred to our obsession to drink and that was an end to it. Far be it from me to admit to any other form of insanity at that point, or even to consider what is now an obvious fact, that there are many forms of insanity, more than I was willing to consider, even after I had seen first-hand the very worst form of alcoholic insanity.

Three or four years prior to my Step One experience, I found myself in one of the treatment settings I mentioned earlier. Try to picture this, if you will. The tenth floor of a rectangular wing of a certain Veterans Hospital. The end one-third of this floor is a day room. Leading from the center of this room, the full length of the rest of the wing is a long, dark hall. This hall is dark because the doors to the rooms on either side of it are kept closed and locked; therefore no light can enter the hall. At the end of the hall is a large double door made of steel, with a very large padlock that prevents anyone's entering or leaving without the use of the key. The rooms on either side of the hall closest to the day room are the nurses' station, surrounded with wire-reinforced glass, and a dining room kept locked except at meal time. The next room on the nurses' station side of the hall is an office and exam room. Next is a shower room which we will discuss later. The remainder of the rooms are patient rooms, with the exception of a locked cleaning supply room.

The day room is equipped with a ping pong table, some card tables and chairs, a small pool table, and various pieces of lounge furniture. It is also equipped with patients in various degrees of distress, from serious to hopeless.

The place is staffed, as nearly as I am able to tell, by nurses, orderlies, student nurses, possibly a social worker, a psychologist who spends his time at the pool table, and a psychiatrist who has the cruelest eyes I have ever looked into. This last is, as nearly as I can tell, the person in charge. Surely she must answer to someone, somewhere; but, if not, then I know in my heart she will one day answer to God. If ever there has been a person who cared nothing for human suffering, here is that person.

As for the patients, there is a man who is tall, elderly and as dignified looking as a man can be in the humiliating clothes that are issued to patients. This man never speaks. In twenty-two days, I have not heard him speak. He usually sits in a lounge chair towards the far corner of the day room; quite suddenly he will stand and, one piece at a time, divest himself of his clothing. He will remain undressed until one or two of the more fortunate patients dress him again. He can't do it himself, though he makes a small effort to, because he is nearly blind and doesn't know a shirt from a pair of pants since they are made of the same material. Shortly after he has been helped back to his chair, he will rise and repeat the procedure. This will continue throughout the day, every day, all day long.

Two sides of this day room open to an outside view through windows that run the entire length of the room. Near the windows on one side sits a gray-haired man who never leaves his chair, except for meals or bed time or other necessities. This man, like the other, does not speak, with this exception: every twenty minutes or so, in a loud, rather raspy baritone voice, he calls out, "Cigarette, please . . . cigarette, please . . . cigarette, please . . . " and continues until one less unfortunate goes to him, lights a cigarette and holds it while he smokes. As he smokes, he may make a bit of meaningless small talk until his helper tells him the cigarette is finished and has to be extinguished. Then he thanks the person pleasantly; twenty minutes or so later you hear, "Cigarette, please . . . cigarette, please . . . cigarette, please . . . " all day long until bedtime, every day.

There sits a man reading a book. He enjoys his book and likes to talk about it and other books he has read. He willingly lends a book if someone expresses interest in it. A very pleasant man. Until bedtime. At bedtime, all patients leave the day room together and go to the shower room. At this, the very pleasant man who likes to read books goes berserk. A shower is a must; it is one of the rules. This man screams, kicks, bites, hits, and swears to avoid the shower. It takes more than one or two people to force him into the shower. He immediately settles down after his shower, puts on his regulation pajamas and goes quietly to bed. Why? No one knows. But in such a setting, there is always one who, out of boredom or cursedness, steps up to this man as he sits quietly reading, and leaning close, says in a loud voice, "Shower time!" The perpetrator jumps back as the man begins cursing and screaming, continuing until reassured that it is not shower time.

All here are addressed as Mister this or that, except "Shorty." Shorty is called Shorty for the obvious reason that he is shorter than the average American male by a considerable measurement, and because he has an endearing personality that causes you to want to befriend him. Shorty wears his snow-white hair in a crew cut and is further distinguished from others by his slippers, which are sheep-lined leather with soft soles that swish, swish, swish, as he shuffles about the room over the tiled floor. Shorty looks out the window, comments on the weather, watches a game of pool being played when the psychologist does not have the table tied up for his own entertainment, stands and watches a card game or ping pong game, wanders back to the windows, comments on the weather, and then shoves his hands in his pockets and wanders off down that long, black hall, calling, "Mom . . . oh, Mom . . . Mom . . . oh, Mom . . . Mom . . . oh, Mom . . . " in a loud voice that fades away and then increases again in volume as he returns, still calling for Mom, whom he will never find.

Meanwhile, we are given the opportunity to become better acquainted with the psychiatrist, which we regret. Here is a very angry person with little or no compassion for, and a lot less understanding of, the problems and feelings of the residents. When she interviews, as apparently she must, she snaps her questions and demands answers whether there be sensible answers or no answers. I have seen live rattlesnakes rather close-up, and they have no more venomous look in their reptilian eye than this woman in charge of the care of several men. In her presence, I feel at all times and in all ways hated passionately. Several years later, I will learn that this is indeed so and at the same time learn why. Meanwhile, I'm scared to death of her.

One day, the nursing staff comes to me asking a favor. I am told that the staff is short-handed, that one of the men not mentioned above is sick, and that it would be helpful if I would sit with this man. He is in a room at the far end of the hall, in bed with a glucose bottle hung above him and attached to his arm with a needle. What is needed, they say, is that I sit beside him with my hand on his arm to prevent him from moving it and pulling the needle out. I am to notify the staff with a buzzer attached to the head of the bed when the glucose bottle is nearly empty. The man does nothing but breathe while I am with him; his eyelids do not flutter, much less does he move.

In the evening, we are playing a game of cards when a man in a wheelchair is brought into the day room and left facing the television, which is up on the wall out of reach of everyone and controlled from the nursing station. I glance over at the new arrival and am amazed to see that it is the man I sat with throughout the afternoon. I am more than amazed; I am also deeply concerned and keep glancing in his direction as play continues at the table. After a short while, the man's head is tipped back, his mouth is open, and he is staring at the ceiling. He is dead, and no one seems to give a damn. Then I realize that he was expected to die as I sat with him during the afternoon, and since he did not follow the script, he was wheeled out where I would be sure to witness his expiration. Exactly what lesson the good doctor wanted me to learn, I don't know; but the result was that I learned to hate her guts.

It was within her power to keep me there indefinitely, and at times I thought she would. She didn't. Upon my release, a car came to pick me up at the front door of that huge building. I stopped on the sidewalk beside the car and looked up. A man was up there who would disrobe several times this day; another would call out repeatedly for a cigarette; another would go berserk at the word "shower," and another sad little man would continue his search for "Mom" and never find her.

Korsikoff syndrome, Organic Brain Syndrome, or OBS to some "professionals." More commonly, though less kindly, referred to as "wet brain." The ultimate form of alcoholic insanity, from which these men suffered, happens. I have no idea if the men described had ever been offered help, if they had ever heard of AA or had ever been shown a copy of "Alcoholics Anonymous" also known as the Big Book. I only know they were there and that there they would stay until the end, a direct result of the constant, heavy use of alcohol.

Step Two does not tell us we must believe in God. It simply says, "Came to believe that a Power . . . " and it does not say immediately, overnight, or in fact any particular time. So if you have that hang-up, get rid of it. Now.

A young fellow came to me once saying he was an atheist and could not get anywhere with Step Two because of his not believing in a higher power. All the suggestions I made seemed to bring about stronger resistance until we were both frustrated. We worked on the problem for several days together, and then he came into my office and asked, "Do you think I can use TRUTH for a higher power?" Bingo! That was his answer, and to the best of my knowledge, it is working to this day.

Another man claimed his higher power to be a lamp post because he said that was what held him up when he was drunk. He was obviously not serious, but one way or the other it didn't work. He relapsed.

Concentrate on your own insanity. Begin to develop a brutally honest concept of yourself so that when the time comes to ask for help you know what, exactly, to ask for. It would also be a good idea to know how to ask.

Step Three is meant to help with both the what and how, but mostly the how.

symptom→ALCHOLE is NOT PROBLEM
SELF is, 5 CHP - BIG BOOK

STEP ONE

We admitted we were powerless over WHATEVER our problem is, that our FEELINGS had become unmanageable.

STEP TWO

Came to believe THAT a power greater than ourselves could restore us to sanity.

Remember, it is THAT a power, not IN a power, and the emphasis of our thought should be on the word SANITY.

NOTES

SELF is PROBELM; ALCOHOL IS A
symptiom.
SELF WILL NOT GOD'S WILL; WHEN I CHOOSE
MY WILL OUT OF THINKING NOT FEELING
THAT GOD CAN'T OR WON'T SEE TO MY NEEDS
DON'T TRUST THAT GOD; KNOW WHAT IS BEST FOR
ME OR HE DOSE AND WON'T; OR HE CAN'T.
But HE CAN & WILL IF I SEEK HIM
By PRACTICING THE 12 STEPS.

Step Three

MADE A DECISION TO TURN OUR WILL AND OUR LIFE OVER TO THE CARE OF GOD AS WE UNDERSTOOD HIM

A drunk was walking along the street with one foot on the side walk and one in the gutter when a cop stopped him: "Hey, Mister! You're drunk!" "D'ya rilly think sho, Offisher?" "I sure do!" "Gee, I'm gladda hear that, I thought I wash crippled!"

I read a poster once that said, "Not To Decide Is To Decide." I read it several times before I caught on. I'll let you think about it for a while before I share my interpretation.

Maybe we ought to take a look at a definition of "decision" before we continue. Decision. n. a making up of one's mind (the result of making up one's mind; the judge's decision is final); resoluteness (The New Lexicon Webster's Dictionary of the English Language). There. That should sufficiently cloud the issue. Nothing like complicating things, is there? The decision-making process in this step is really very simple, but not necessarily very easy. We hold back because of a natural fear of change, a fear of failure, a fear of the unknown—and because of an inflated ego that insists on telling us that we can handle this problem without spiritual help.

God wants to be your friend, so why not decide to let Him?

Of course, we cover all this with a good coating of bravado by saying things like, "Don't go giving me a bunch of that God stuff; I had enough of that jammed down my throat when I was a kid," and other similar remarks that are meant to hold anyone at bay who may be trying to encourage us to take a new approach to a troubled and often broken life.

But let's take a common-sense look at where we are and where we are headed. Let's see if we don't believe change, if not desirable, is absolutely necessary in order to get our train back on track.

What are we being asked to do? Someone is suggesting that we let go of a lot of heavy problems and find solutions to them. The things we have tried in the past haven't worked. So someone comes along, offers something different, and we balk with all our might, especially at the idea that we may become religious. I suggest you can be religious about anything and in fact, you are and have always been. For example, you can be a religious drinker, a religious smoker, a religious eater, a religious lover, a religious football fan (fan means fanatic, after all). We can be religious about our jobs, religious complainers, religious gossips, and . . . . I think I've made the point.

So I suggest it is time to stop deciding not to decide, which means to do nothing, to accept things as they are no matter how messed up they may seem because they are what we are accustomed to. We are more comfortable with unhappiness than we are with the idea of making some real, honest-to-goodness changes. Oh, we want the change, but we want someone to do it for us. We want them to do it right now, the idea of gradual growth suggesting things like effort, thought, and maybe something a little bit painful.

If you have accepted your powerlessness, your unmanageability, and your insanity, and if you believe or if you want to believe that a power greater than yourself can help you, then it is decision time. Simple, but not easy. Maybe your past teachings, or the lack of them, have made you a skeptic, but that doesn't prevent you from making a decision. Leave religion out of it, forget what you learned in the past, and simply decide there must be a better way.

My own religious background is a hodgepodge, a mixture of denominational teachings, bigotry, and other sundry junk. Just fine for some people but never very helpful to me. I attended a Swedish Lutheran Sunday School as a child until I was six years old. Then I attended Sunday School at a church called the First Christian Church, then at a church called the Congregational, then the Baptist Church. I heard the "old time religion" at the Swedish Lutheran where, as a very little boy, I learned that naughty boys go to hell. Since I knew I was naughty (we all have consciences, you know), I knew exactly where I was going, because I heard that place described quite vividly on many Sunday mornings.

So, God was no friend of mine. I went to all those different denominational groups because my parents, due to what is sometimes called "the Great Depression," moved from one town to another, or one neighborhood to another, while my father looked for ways to support a wife and three kids. I learned, to my surprise, when I was thirty-seven years old, that my parents were Methodists. At that time I still knew I was "naughty" even though I was no longer a little boy (I was a little boy inside), and I still was deeply concerned about what God had in mind for me.

FEELINGS ARE NEITHER GOOD OR BAD
THOUGHTS ARE + DECISIONS ARE + MY WILL IS!

Therefore, Step Three was not easy. Just simple. With my background, I had to do a lot of heavy thinking. A fellow told me once, "get down on your knees and stay there until you get an answer." Good idea if you know the question. I had to figure that out first. What is decision? What is will? What is life? How do I turn this over to the care of God? What do I understand of God? Obviously my understanding of God was practically nil. Still is. Who understands God? Nobody. So get off the hang-up. What does the step tell me to do? Let go and let God. So do it.

One thing I did learn and believe was that life came from God. When I finally realized that life is feelings, it led to the questions of "what is my will?" and "where did it come from?"

If you go to an attorney to make out a will, what are you doing? You are making a legal document stating what you want done after your demise. What you want done. What you want. Will is want. Read the step this way. Made a decision to turn my wants (plural because I have more than one want) and my feelings over to the care of God as I did not understand him. Might as well keep it honest.

Your feelings come first. God gave them to you because you are human, and some of them are not very nice. But they are real, and they are an important part of you that will have to be faced honestly. Humbling? Yes. Humiliating? Not necessarily; it depends on how you personally look at it. Humble is not thinking less of yourself, it is just thinking of yourself less.

Your feelings cause your wants. How do you know when you need food? You are hungry. Hunger is a feeling. How do you know when you need sleep? You feel it. How do you know when you want to make love? You feel it. Feel, feel, feel, constantly feeling; want, want, want, constantly wanting.

Now, it stands to reason if your feelings have become unmanageable, your wants have become unmanageable. Consequently, your behavior has become unmanageable, hence the need to be restored to sanity. So what do you do? What will God do? And how will He do it?

First of all, if you have compared what your life has been and is to what you want it to be, you ask God to help you with each little problem as it comes along. Ask Him in English. Modern English. He gave you a language, so use it.

This is not meant to be a Bible lesson, but I need to refer to the Bible right now anyway. The Bible says that God is our father. I am the father of two children, and I love them. So I can, from that, assume that God loves me. I enjoy hearing from my children, talking with them. I hear their voice on the phone and immediately get a warm fuzzy. You know what that is. It's the opposite of a cold prickly. So I think when God hears me talking with Him, He gets a warm fuzzy.

But if my kids called me up only to complain and whine, I'd not enjoy it nearly so much as I do. I like to hear about the good things. And if they called and sounded like I have heard some people sound when praying, I wouldn't enjoy that either, and I'm talking about old English. "Hi Dadeth. How art thou doingeth? I just calledeth to sayeth helloeth and telleth youeth that I misseth youeth."

I'd call the nearest place to them that I could find to see if I could get them some help, if it wasn't already too late. So would you. So why talk that way to God? He wouldn't understandeth anywayeth.

Here is the way Step Three works. You've got a problem, large or small. You have feelings about the problem. You want it resolved. Feelings and wants. You try to resolve it. You fail. You ask God to take care of it, your feelings about it, and what you want done about it. Then you wait. Nothing happens. Ask again. Still nothing. Then you decide God didn't hear you, or that God doesn't care. So you ask Him again. And again. Spell pray backward, what do you get? I get yarp. So are we praying or yarping? The trouble is that you are leaving something out that is of utmost importance in getting help with a problem. People.

God works through people. Consider your shoes. I will assume they are made of leather. Someone, somewhere, is raising a cow that will be transported to market by someone, received by someone, butchered by someone, skinned by someone; the hide will be tanned by someone, transported to a shoe factory by someone, cut to a pattern by someone, stitched together by someone, inspected by someone, packed by someone, transported by someone, stored in a warehouse by someone, shipped again by someone, received by someone, put on a shelf by someone, sold to you by someone. (After all that you are going to complain to someone that your feet hurt.)

There are a lot of someones involved in taking care of your feet. Same goes for your other clothing, your toiletries, food, recreational toys; the list is practically endless.

The same is true of your other problems. God will help with them, but you need to involve people, and you need to use common sense. For some problems you go to a banker, for some a lawyer, a grocer, a minister, a counselor, a friend and, in the above example, a shoe salesperson.

I spent many years stumbling along, thinking I was crippled, with one foot in an alcoholic gutter. If I had made the decision called for in step three, I very possibly would have fallen into that gutter and died there.

Compare the power of God to the power supply in your home. I don't know about you, but when I walk into a dark room, I get a sort of uneasy feeling and that feeling makes me want light. So, I make a decision to find the light switch. Electricity has been at that switch all along, but it couldn't get to the light bulb because the switch has been open, meaning there has been a gap that the electricity couldn't cross, just like a locomotive that comes to a gap in the railroad track can't proceed. So I flip the switch closing the gap, the current proceeds to the bulb, enters, crosses the filament creating light, and proceeds to the ground. If there is no ground, the electricity can't go on. I'm still in the dark.

You have a problem (lack of power). You ask God (the power source) and that action on your part closes the switch, allowing the power to flow as long as you have the whole thing properly grounded. Your problem may be hunger or it may be any other feeling, and you can talk to God about it. But if you don't talk to people, then there is no ground. The power stops and you're still in the dark. In other words, without other people, we're going to be hungry. God works through people. He will work through you, because sometimes there are things no one can do for you. The next step is one of those.

STEP ONE

We admitted we were powerless over WHATEVER our problem is, that our FEELINGS had become unmanageable.

STEP TWO

Came to believe THAT a power greater than ourselves could restore us to SANITY.

STEP THREE

Made a decision to turn our WANTS and our FEELINGS over to the care of God even though we may not understand Him.

If you don't close the switch so your prayer is grounded, the results may be minimal. Remember—God works through people. This step involves trusting the right people. It also depends a lot on whether you are praying or yarping. God wants to be your friend and a friend is someone who knows you and likes you anyway.

NOTES

Step Four

MADE A SEARCHING, FEARLESS, MORAL INVENTORY OF OURSELVES

O wad some Power the giftie gie us
To see oursels as ithers see us;
It wad frae monie a blunder free us,
An' foolish notion.
What airs in dress an' gait wad lea'e us.
An' ev'n devotion!

—Robert Burns

Here is a step that is marvelous in its simplicity and frightening in its difficulty. This is the first of the steps in which we are required not only to use our intellect but also to do a written assignment. When it is explained, we find it simple but gut-wrenching. We are about to practice what has been referred to as rigorous honesty—on paper, where we will see it.

The word honesty is so important here that I am tempted to reword the step itself, to use the word honest in place of moral. Made a searching, fearless, HONEST inventory of ourselves. I don't particularly care for the word moral anyway, because we have been moralized, scandalized, scorned and pitied quite enough in the past, while no one who was on the other end of all that was able to help us. Many tried their best and many are no longer willing to even try. We are going to have to do this thing ourselves.

When I think about it, I am reminded of a message I read a long time ago to this effect: "I have been held up, held down, walked on, bulldozed, blackjacked, cheated, squeezed and mooched, struck for war tax, excess profits tax, per capita tax, state tax, county tax, sales tax and dog tax, asked to help the society of John the Baptist, GAR, men's relief, women's relief and stomach relief and to donate to the Red Cross, Green Cross and double cross; and because I wouldn't spend or lend all the little I earn and go beg, borrow or steal, I have been cussed and discussed, talked to, talked about, and darn near trimmed and ruined and the only reason I'm sticking around now is to see what the hell is coming next." So much then, for the word moral.

Honesty is the key to our future happiness, serenity and peace of mind. It is absolutely necessary to the successful continuance of this program, and it does not come easily nor does it come right away. But for the purpose of Step Four, it is time to do your dead-level best to be strictly honest with yourself and hope for continued improvement in the future.

What is an inventory? It is an accounting of all that is good and bad, a method of discovering the condition of things. If we are talking about a business, where this term is used most and the principles of accounting most often put into practice, then we are considering things like stock on hand, accounts receivable, cash on hand, furniture, fixtures and equipment, buildings, land, and so on, or any other assets, such as stocks, bonds, various types of investments and what have you. Then it is also necessary to account for all spoiled goods, accounts payable, deterioration of furniture, fixtures, land. All this is to prepare a balance sheet to show the condition of business at the close of business on some certain date. In the case of businesses, this may be somewhat easier in this age of computers than it once was, because a running inventory can be kept and the accountant can give the condition of the business almost at a moment's notice.

In talking about a human being, the human condition is not going to be any more easily ascertained than a business. As far as Step Four is concerned, we are not to the age of computers as yet. That age will come when we arrive at Step Ten. For now, we will do it the old-fashioned way, but we will still be looking for a balance—a balanced condition. To properly take inventory, assets must be considered as well as liabilities. It is important to be aware of that right now. An honest inventory cannot be an honest inventory if all it takes into account is the "bad." When you finish with a fourth step personal inventory and the next step, "Admitted to God, to ourselves and to another human being the exact nature of our wrongs," you should be feeling good about yourself. Therefore, we are going to look at all we can think of that is good about ourselves. Again: "Self acceptance is the name of the game!"

But first, before we look at our "goodies," we need to deal with the things about ourselves that have bothered us for years.

Let's get to the how-to's.

Get a notebook. Make it a small, inexpensive notebook because you are not going to be writing a letter or a journal, you are going to throw it away when you have completed Step Five. No one else is going to read this inventory. It is yours and it is private. So you can stop worrying now about your handwriting or your spelling. I want to emphasize, throw it away (or shred and recycle it) when you are finished, after Step Five, that is. I knew a man who kept it, thinking he had it hidden. You cannot hide something from your wife in her own house. She found and read it, and it nearly cost them their marriage.

Open the notebook to a page somewhere near the back and write in detail the thing you consider to be the worst thing you have ever done. This has nothing to do with what you believe others may think; it has to do only with your most secret, private, hidden thing. Write in detail. I repeat: in detail. But remember, this is your inventory, your story, your past. If and when it is necessary at any place therein to use another's name, use only initials unless the other person being mentioned is entirely innocent of any blame regarding what you are writing about.

The reason I suggest that you write out the worst thing first is very simple. A long time ago, I heard a woman say: "Do the thing you fear the most and the death of fear is certain." Think about it. Once the worst is out, the rest will be much easier for you.

You will be considering the following:

Selfishness, alibis (excuses), pride, intolerance, envy, fear, lust, dishonest thinking, resentment, impatience, self pity, phoniness, laziness, gluttony.

Open your notebook, leaving the first two or three pages blank for the sake of privacy, and write each of the above at the top of a page by itself. Selfishness at the top of a page, dishonest thinking at the top of a page, and so on. This will amount to your outline.

You will also be writing examples of having broken the Ten Commandments.

"I am the Lord, thy God. Thou shalt have no other Gods before me. Thou shalt not take the name of the Lord thy God in vain. Remember the Sabbath Day, to keep it holy. Honor thy father and thy mother. Thou shalt not kill. Thou shalt not commit adultery. Thou shalt not steal. Thou shalt nor bear false witness against thy neighbor. Thou shalt not covet thy neighbor's wife. Thou shalt not covet thy neighbor's goods."

Write each one at the top of a page by itself. Don't start making excuses ("I never did that"), because you did do it and it needs to be written at the top of a page as a part of this inventory. "Well, I never killed anybody." You have never, in anger, wished someone were dead? Come on, write it at the top of the page. Quit stalling, we're being honest here. I never said it would be easy.

This, then, is the outline for the first part of the step. This part deals with the "bad," the "liabilities" side of the ledger. Look at it this way: "I'm gonna take myself apart and fix me." This is the taking apart. Later you will put yourself back together in a much better working order.

Think about your life. The places you have lived, the places you have worked, where you went to school, the people you have known. Remember as far back as you can. Every time you think of something that bothers you, that you feel guilty about, ashamed of, wish you hadn't done, ask yourself this question: "Why did I do that?" Look at your outline or the above list of character defects. What was the cause of your behavior? One or more of those character defects was the underlying cause of the action, because (Step One) it had become unmanageable.

Incidentally, the Ten Commandments do not cause behavior. They regulate it or judge it. So just refer to the character defects. When you decide the cause of the behavior in question, write out what you did in detail on the page under the appropriate heading.

Let me give you an example.

I was about four years old. I conned my mother out of a nickel to go to a little store nearby and buy candy. Nickels were hard to come by in those days; the Great Depression was in full swing. But I told Mom I would buy a Snickers bar and bring it home to share with her. In those days, Snickers bars came two in a package. So I knew I could get two for the price of one. I remember after buying the candy, I was leaving the store and I was already opening the wrapper. When I was half way home, my share of the candy had been eaten. I looked at Mom's candy bar and said to myself that she wouldn't care if I took one bite of hers. In those exact words. When I got home there was no candy because one bite led to another and so on.

I don't remember what happened then. I only remember that I ate it all. For many, many years afterward I felt guilty every time I saw a Snickers bar. So when I was in my thirties, I bought a candy bar and drove one hundred miles to give it to Mom. She said, "Oh, that's nice, why did you do that?" When I explained, she did not remember the incident at all. As the little boy on TV said, "Moms are like that; yeah, they are."

I am using this example for several reasons. One is that it demonstrates that I hope you will go back as far as possible in your memory. Another is that it demonstrates we are taking an inventory of our behavior whether we were drinking or not. Then, as you will see, it uncovers a multitude of sins.

Now look through the list of character defects above. What do you think, of fifteen character defects, was the cause of my behavior in this example? I'm going to write it out under gluttony, remembering that no one is going to see this but me. I don't have to worry about neatness, spelling or anything but to GET THE DETAILS ON PAPER. The page in my notebook might look like this:

GLUTTONY

> I was abt 4 yrs old. I conned Mom o/of 5c to by candy to share with her. I bot it at a little place close to home. I 8 it all b4 I got home.

That takes care of it does it not? It does not. There is much more involved than gluttony. Under the paragraph above I would need to write this word: ALSO.

The example might end by looking like this:

GLUTTONY

> I was abt 4 yrs old. I conned Mom o/of 5c to by candy to share with her. I bot it at a little place close to home. I 8 it all b 4 I got home. ALSO—selfishness, alibis (she wouldn't care if I took one bite of hers), dishonest thinking, impatience, phoniness (it was a con from the word go), and I broke the fourth commandment, the seventh commandment and the tenth commandment.

What I hope you will do is scrutinize your entire life, looking for examples. To be effective, this inventory should have no less than two specific (detailed) examples under each heading, more if you feel the need. Each example should be different. It would be ineffective to use the same example in different places.

What I now want to point out to you is very important. The step says we took an inventory of—OURSELVES! It does NOT say we took an inventory of our behavior. We are taking an inventory of our character defects (the causes of our behavior). This is not going to lead to a confessional, but is, instead, an evaluation of our personality.

Now to the assets, or "fix me" part. What we do now should create the "balance sheet," the "condition of the business" at the end of the period. Your character assets are the tools that you have to work with.

I believe one of my favorite songs of all time is *Inchworm*. If you don't know it or don't remember it, here are the words:

Inchworm, inchworm,
Measuring the marigolds.
You and your arithmetic—
You really should go far.

Inchworm, inchworm
Measuring the marigolds
Seems to me you'd stop to see
How beautiful they are.

You have been measuring yourself. Now take time to see how beautiful you are, because you really are beautiful, no matter what you may have been thinking of yourself. I recall a time years back when I had really messed things up, and I was feeling down on myself. Really down. I came to my desk and found there a bank check. It was blank, so I turned it over and there on the back I found this message:

> "When is the time to love a man the most? When he's done things good, and made everybody happy? Then you ain't done learnin' yet, 'cause that ain't the time at all. It's when he's at his lowest, and can't believe in hisself 'cause the world done whupped him so. When you measure a man, measure him right, child, measure him right. Be sure you done taken into account all the hills and valleys he's come through to get wherever he's at."
>
> –Raisin In The Sun

I still have that note. It is a reminder from a friend that I am human and need not be so hard on myself.

Measure yourself by the ruler below.

Assets are such feelings or traits, if you will, as the following:

Faith, love, cheerfulness, loyalty, punctuality, caution in speech, patience, integrity, gratitude, hope, courtesy, order, use of time, sincerity, kindness, tolerance, balance.

The reason I refer to them as feelings or traits is that you are going to write a paragraph telling HOW YOU FEEL NOW (because how you feel at any given moment is who you are) about each of these characteristics. You will not give examples of things you've done in the past that relate to each of these; that would be on the borderline of boasting and if I'm right, you can't afford to boast. This part of the inventory is a guide to what you can become.

In writing how you FEEL NOW, be honest. Examine yourself as you approach each topic. Be done with phoniness. If, for example, at the time of writing you believe for some reason of your own that courtesy is an attitude for worms, then write something like, "I feel that courtesy is wormy." Just tell the truth; don't try to present yourself as something you are not.

And now, as we approach the end, consider attitudes and responsibilities. What is your attitude now toward God, yourself, your family, your work, your friends, your neighbors, your community? Write a few words telling how YOU FEEL about each of those, and then write what you believe your responsibilities are to each of those.

Whew! You are finished. I hope you have just finished the most honest thing you have ever done in your lifetime. If you have, and no one knows but you, you will be rewarded in time with happiness, serenity, and peace of mind. That is, if you continue with the rest of the steps.

Don't quit now!

STEP ONE

We admitted we were powerless over WHATEVER our problem is, that our FEELINGS had become unmanageable.

STEP TWO

Came to believe THAT a power greater than ourselves could restore us to SANITY.

STEP THREE

Made a decision to turn our WANTS and our FEELINGS over to the care of God even though we may not understand Him.

STEP FOUR

Made a searching, SCARY, HONEST inventory of ourselves.

If you are now working on your inventory, be as honest as possible with both the liabilities and the assets. Don't cheat yourself out of the good stuff, neither present yourself as better than you are. This is YOUR inventory and it is you who is on the road to happiness, serenity, and peace of mind.

NOTES

Step Five

ADMITTED TO GOD, TO OURSELVES, AND TO ANOTHER HUMAN BEING, THE EXACT NATURE OF OUR WRONGS

A man drunker than a skunk was leaning out of the second floor window of a hotel. He leaned too far and fell. Fortunately for him, the hotel awning was open directly below him. He landed on the awning, rolled off and hit the gutter.

Quickly a small crowd gathered; one fellow looked down at the drunk and said, "Gosh, mister, what happened?"

The drunk replied, "I don't know; I just got here too."

Recalling the first time I went through this step would be embarrassing if I had not learned by now to accept my past, forgive myself for it, and put it where it belongs. The past is the past. But I remember it nevertheless, and I am free to say it was a sad waste of time for the clergyman who had been chosen to listen to me and for myself as well. Since I know God was listening, I imagine He was saying, "Yuuccch!"

For one thing, I had only skimmed the surface in doing the fourth step; for another, I was not willing to be honest; for another, I was afraid of what the minister might think of me; and for one more, I was afraid and unwilling to look at myself. Furthermore, I did not want to let go of some of my character defects.

This mockery of the fifth step took place at a treatment center, and I had no one fooled. The man assigned as my counselor, with tears in his eyes because he really cared, tried his best to get me to stay in treatment on an extended care basis. Otherwise, I was scheduled to leave the next day, and he knew that my chances of any sort of recovery were nil. But I refused to stay. Four days later, I was too drunk to hit the ground with my hat.

The Man in the Glass

When you get what you want from the struggle for self
  and the world makes you king for a day,

Just go to a mirror and look at yourself
and see what that man has to say.
For it isn't your father or mother or wife
who judgment upon you must pass,
The fellow whose verdict counts most in your life
is the man staring back from the glass.
He's the fellow to please, never mind all the rest,
for he's with you right up to the end,
And you've passed your most dangerous, difficult test
if the man in the glass is your friend.
Though others may call you a square shootin' chum
and say you're a wonderful guy,
The man in the glass says you're only a bum
if you can't look him right in the eye.
You can fool the whole world down the pathway of years
and get pats on the back as you pass,
But your final reward will be heartaches and tears
if you've cheated the man in the glass.

—Anonymous

I had fooled no one. I had cheated myself. But this is today—and I just got here.

The next and last time I approached this step was different. I was afraid to face the minister because he was a friend of mine and a friend of my friends. Oh, how I hated telling him the things I had to say. I suspect I would have hated it even had he not been a friend, because far be it from me to ever say that self-disclosure is easy. But do you know what? It didn't phase him. He didn't put his hand over his mouth and stare at me as if I were some kind of freak. He didn't throw up when I told him what I thought was the worst thing I ever did.

It won't be that way for you either. You will find, if you begin with the worst thing first, the thing you fear most to share, that as you go along you will have a pleasant experience of self-acceptance and acceptance by another human being. You will experience freedom as you have not felt it in a long time. In the process, you are very apt to make friends with God.

The following story about a quite famous man was told to me as being true. He was dying in a hospital when a minister who had heard about it came to his bedside and, leaning over close to him, asked in a concerned voice if he had made his peace with God. The dying man's answer was simply, "I didn't know we were at odds."

That man was at peace. What a nice way to feel about the end of things as we know them—at peace with God, with ourselves and with humanity; no deep, dark, hidden secrets to carry away with us; free from the worry of being "found out," of facing God with unfinished business, having left our yesterdays behind, looking forward to a peaceful eternity.

Steps Four, Five, Six, Seven, Eight, and Nine are the beginning of that kind of life. Step Four is a written inventory; Step Five is a verbal inventory in which we talk about the things in our character that need "fixing." It, too, is a scary step. But you have come this far, and it would be a real tragedy if you stopped now.

The most important word in Step Five is the word "exact." The "exact" nature of our wrongs. It would be easy, I think, to become a bit confused at this point. So let's get it straight now and avoid all confusion. When you wrote your personal inventory in Step Four, you wrote about things you have done that have been harmful to others as well as to yourself. But you were not taking inventory of what you have done, but rather of who you have been.

You were using examples of what you have done to get at the "cause" of your behavior. We are dealing with cause and effect. In the example I used in Step Four, I was showing that gluttony and other character defects were the cause of my behavior in eating my mother's share of the candy. Gluttony was the exact nature of my wrong, along with the other defects named.

So in Step Five, we are looking at the character defects as the "exact" nature of our wrongs. Those are the things we want to talk about, backing them up with the examples we have written. You should have your written fourth step with you, look at it for notes, and say out loud to another human being the things you have discovered about yourself.

Turn to the back of your inventory where you have stored the "worst thing you have ever done" and tell it to the person who is listening to you. Now you realize how important it is that the person you choose to hear your fifth step is a person you can trust completely. I always recommend a minister and preferably one who has some background or training in fifth step work, one who realizes that all he is expected to do is to be a pair of ears, not judgmental, just willing to listen, period.

A minister cannot be forced in a court of law to testify against you, and most ministers have taken an oath that will guarantee confidentiality. So, you have the comfort of privacy and for that you should be grateful.

Once you have talked about the "worst thing," proceed with the rest of your fourth step material as you have it written.

"Admitted to God"—God already knows. "To ourselves"—our self already knows. "To another human being." Out of the darkness, into the light. That spells relief. The amazing thing is, it really is a relief, a lasting one at that. I heard a fellow say, "I didn't know, and I didn't know that I didn't know." But now, for sure, you know because you have written it, and you have talked about it. It is in the past and done with.

The fifth step is a kind of prayer in the presence of another human who is, believe it or not, also imperfect and will probably surprise you with the amount of understanding they show.

I say it is a kind of prayer because there is more to it than "the exact nature of our wrongs." You are talking to God. You are telling Him the things that you have kept secret, in some cases, even from yourself. I hope you will also talk to Him about the other side of the ledger. The good stuff. It's kind of like saying, "God, this is the way I was, but I feel this way about it now." Then talk about HOW YOU FEEL concerning the character assets (the "good" stuff) that you wrote in the second part of your fourth step. Read what you wrote if you want to, but read it out loud.

Now if someone asks you if you have made your peace with God, you can answer, "I didn't know we were at odds." What a pleasant feeling it is. You are going to walk with a lighter step, a brighter smile and a new attitude toward yourself and your fellow man.

Now if you really want to dump the junk that has burdened your life, look at the sixth step.

STEP ONE

We admitted we were powerless over WHATEVER our problem is, that our FEELINGS had become unmanageable.

STEP TWO

Came to believe THAT a power greater than ourselves could restore us to SANITY.

STEP THREE

Made a decision to turn our WANTS and our FEELINGS over to the care of God even though we may not understand Him.

STEP FOUR

Made a searching, SCARY, HONEST inventory of ourselves.

STEP FIVE

Admitted to God, to ourselves and another human being the EXACT nature of our wrongs.

The EXACT nature of our wrongs is the CAUSE of our wrongs, the UNMANAGEABLE CHARACTER DEFECTS that dictated our behavior. If we have openly discussed each of these, we need never again worry about Step Five, even though we may not have talked about everything we did wrong. Step Five is not a confessional but is a self-evaluation.

NOTES

Step Six

WERE ENTIRELY READY TO HAVE GOD REMOVE ALL THESE DEFECTS OF CHARACTER

The Step One experience. Remember the pain? Remember hating yourself? Remember the shame, guilt and remorse? I should think by now, and especially so if you have done your fourth and fifth steps well, that you are feeling somewhat better about yourself. Maybe, and I hope this is so, you are feeling a great deal better about yourself, that maybe the person in the mirror isn't so bad after all—a person you might just learn to live with in peace.

Now, as you approach Step Six, I wonder if you are entirely ready—entirely ready—to have God remove your character defects. Are you? Think about it. If your Step One experience was anything at all like mine, then at that time you were entirely ready to let go of any and all, even though you weren't aware of exactly what was wrong. But now you are feeling better after your Step Five experience, and it may be easier to say the words than to feel the need.

Character means personality. Look at it this way: personality characteristics. Part of you. So what I'm asking is, "are you willing to change who you are?" Remember, you have been you for a long time. Even though you may not like you very much, the question is almost bound to come to mind, "who will I be when I stop being who I have been?"

I heard a speaker once who ended her talk with the following:

> "Lord, I ain't what I ought to be,
> And Lord, I ain't what I want to be,
> And Lord, I ain't what I'm going to be,
> But thank you, Lord, I ain't what I used to be."

In my case I was ready for a junk yard. Sometimes I think about God as kind of a junk dealer who goes through the junk yards of the world looking for things He might salvage. When He came to where I was, He picked me up, rubbed me off on His sleeve a little bit, blew

His breath on me, polished me on His sleeve again, and said to Himself, "I think maybe I can use this thing," and took me away from there. In due time, He began restoration.

Have you ever rebuilt an old car or refinished a piece of old furniture? It takes time, patience, and tools, to say nothing of know-how. But the important thing is that it can be done. A piece of junk can be made into something worthwhile.

The Junk Dealer

An old piece of junk, long ago cast aside,
Had once been a treasure, an object of pride.
Passed on hand to hand and no longer in use,
Dented and tarnished from years of abuse
'Til some careless person just tossed it away,
Mindless of what it had been in its day.

So there, in a junk heap, all dusty it lay
Until an old junk dealer happened that way
And picking it up from the dirt and the grime
He saw what a treasure it was in its time
And knew that with time he could surely restore
The beauty and luster of ages before.

The earth is a junkyard of human debris,
Of people who aren't what they wanted to be,
Of people with dreams that have vanished away
And hopes that have died at the end of each day.
The days of their dignity, purpose and pride
Were lost as humanity cast them aside.

But God, looking through all the junk heaps of earth,
Instead of the junk, sees a person of worth.
He sees all the dreams and the hopes that have died
And all of the tears that these children have cried.
And who knows what glory He may have in mind
For the pieces of junk He happens to find?

He loves all His children, not just you and me
And none of us are what He wants us to be.
But down through the ages the story's been told
He will bring His lost sheep back into the fold.
He said of the broken, the fallen, downcast
"The last shall be first and the first shall be last."

By Vaughn

So examine the character defects. Are they all "bad"? I say yes and no. Yes, when they are unmanageable and dictate the terms of my behavior, definitely yes. "When a man loses control of his thinking, he will soon lose control of his behavior," because his thinking and his behavior are very closely linked. The Holy Bible says, "As a man thinketh, so is he." (That's the King James version. We'll talk about that a bit more in Step Eleven.) But think about anger for a moment. Aren't there times when anger is appropriate? If it weren't so, we would all be speaking German or Japanese, those of us who were allowed to live.

Isn't it very natural to be angry at times? When you were born, some big dude grabbed you by the heels and slapped you on your bare posterior. You didn't even know the son of a bitch and hadn't been in this world long enough to have done anything wrong. Injustice! Besides that you were wet, cold, confused, and scared. Who wouldn't be angry?

That anger is still there inside of you somewhere, and I don't blame you. But that doesn't mean we should go looking for that doctor or mid-wife or whoever it was, with the idea of getting even. Anger can be justified, but only when it is not unreasonable.

So I say no, anger isn't always "bad." Without it as a part, and I believe a natural part, of the character of mankind, this world would be so full of injustice that none of us would want to live here. Anger is a defense against injustice. When it is controlled or managed and given reasonable direction, it is "good." When it is used solely as a means to get our own way, it is "bad."

If there are times when anger is appropriate, isn't it also true at least of some of the other character defects? What about pride? Same thing. No one likes an arrogant, self-centered, egotistical person who has no thought for others, who boasts, monopolizes conversations, demands to be center stage in the spotlight, is selfish and self-seeking.

That can be one definition of pride, but then there is the kind of pride we might rather call self-respect. A person lacking self-respect is very apt to be a loser lacking in self-confidence; sloppy about themselves, their relationships with others, and their work. In 1973, I was told about a third grade boy who had been asked to write an essay by his teacher. What he handed in was: "God made me and God don't make no junk." That is acceptable pride. I have since seen this statement in its corrected form (naturally some intellectual had to get hold of it, correct the grammar and make a poster of it). But I like the kid's way of saying it. "God made me and God don't make no junk." Maybe we should all listen to children.

So an argument can be made in favor of several of the character defects, that they are not defects at all, but assets and an important part of life. Intolerance, impatience and fear all have their place in the necessary scheme of things.

Intolerance because injustice, cruelty, crookedness and evil should not be tolerated. Impatience because procrastination can lead to serious problems in time, some important things not being finished until it is too late to finish them. Fear because we need to fear carelessness, fire, criminals and a lot of things that can be dangerous to mankind.

So I ask again, are you ENTIRELY READY to have God remove all these defects of character? What about lust? Are you entirely ready to have God remove it from you? From now on, are you willing to look at a pretty girl's face, not her body? Are you willing never again to look at the ankles first, then the calves and upward from there before you even know what color her hair is? If you answer yes to this, I go on record as saying you are lying. Don't laugh, girls, I have heard you make remarks such as, "Oh boy, ain't he got cute buns?"

That's been going on ever since Satan seduced Eve in the garden. I read somewhere that Satan was the most beautiful of all the angels. He doesn't try to seduce us by showing himself to be ugly. It wouldn't work. He knows the nature of man, and he gets to man through man's own desires, making them as attractive as they can be made. He came swaggering up to Eve in the garden with his best macho look and said, "Hi, chickie, how ya doin'?" Well, I don't suppose Adam was any slouch for looks either, but he didn't have the smoothness Satan has, because up until this time he didn't need it. There wasn't any competition, you see. But Eve was instantly attracted to this new dude and flattered that he would pay attention to her.

She said, "I'm fine." If she had stopped right there or if she had turned and walked away, things would be a lot different in this world. But she didn't. She opened the door by adding, "How are you?"

Satan jumped right on the opportunity and said, "Hey lady, I'm just great! I was just looking this place over. Nice garden you've got here. Is it yours?"

"Yes," she replied, "God gave it to us."

"Us?" he asked.

"My husband and me."

"Oh. So this whole thing is yours and his?"

"Yes, the whole thing. Well, I guess not the whole thing, but everything except that tree over there, because God said if we eat the fruit from that tree we'll die."

Satan said, “Say whaaaat? Hey, come on, chickie, you’re puttin’ me on.”

“No, I’m not; that’s exactly what God said.”

“Well, guess what, chickie, God’s lyin’ to you. Come over here, I want to show you something.”

They walked over to the tree, and Satan reached up and picked some of the fruit. He blew his breath on it, polished it on his sleeve, looked at it for a few seconds with a smile, took a big bite of it, chewed it with an expression of pleasure, almost rapture, and swallowed it.

“Uummmm, that’s good! Delicious!” Wiping the juice off his chin with his sleeve, he looked down at himself in mock surprise and said, “Look, chickie, I ain’t dead. I ain’t even sick! And I gotta tell ya, this stuff is great! Look how juicy it is! Wonderful, wonderful! (And you thought Lawrence Welk invented that expression.) Here, take a bite,” extending the fruit toward her. “Go on, chickie, take a bite. It won’t hurt you at all. God’s a liar. Go on, just take a little bite . . . ”

And she did. And Adam did. And you did. And I did.

And when they did, and when you did, and when I did, our character defects swung into action, and they’ve been going slam-bang ever since.

So, on to Step Seven; humbly asked Him to remove our shortcomings.

STEP ONE

We admitted we were powerless over WHATEVER our problem is, that our FEELINGS had become unmanageable.

STEP TWO

Came to believe THAT a power greater than ourselves could restore us to SANITY.

STEP THREE

Made a decision to turn our WANTS and our FEELINGS over to the care of God even though we may not understand Him.

STEP FOUR

Made a searching, SCARY, HONEST inventory of ourselves.

STEP FIVE

Admitted to God, to ourselves, and another human being the EXACT nature of our wrongs.

STEP SIX

Were ENTIRELY ready to have God remove ALL these defects of character.

We have NO RESERVATIONS. We have recognized our powerlessness over our problem, (Step One); the insanity of our unmanageable feelings (Step Two); we have decided “I can’t do it,

God can, I think I'll let Him (Step Three); we have searched out and talked about our defects (Steps Four and Five); and now we want to be free of them.

NOTES

Step Seven

HUMBLY ASKED HIM TO REMOVE OUR SHORTCOMINGS

Originally written, "Humbly asked Him on our knees to remove our shortcomings," this step can cause a lot of concern and meets with a lot of resistance. Considering the self-centeredness of our personalities, that is no surprise. Since the cradle, we have been arrogant and demanding, suffering from the "king baby" syndrome, demanding full attention with a crown on our heads and a diaper on the other end. It would almost seem that many of us thought our baby bottle was a scepter. We later exchanged the baby bottle for a bottle of booze.

Then, sick, alone, often frightened, filled with remorse, guilt, and shame, we might cry out to a God we had ignored, denied, and in our drunken haze, even cursed, asking Him to help us through our self-imposed grief, making drunken, sorrowful promises of repentance and renewal that were promptly forgotten the next time Ethyl Alcohol reared her ugly head.

When the ill effects had worn off again, the cycle was broken once again, and we felt better once again. Then we would polish our crown of self-sufficiency and return to our quest of ruling the universe, riding high, wide and handsome on the imaginary stallion of our over-blown self-esteem, a self-made person, a self-made god on his or her way to another meeting with specters that can only be found in a bottle.

Give up. There's a saying, "Let go and let God." Just give up. What are you holding onto? Your reputation? Your successes? Your sweet, kind, loving personality? Your pride? Your family's respect for you? Your loss of jobs? Your having spent all your money? Your loss of friends? Your lying? Your cheating? What are you hanging onto?

Discover a better way of overcoming your character defects than to ask the help of God and you will have found a way to help many people. I balked, too. I didn't want to appear weak even though I knew that I had no strength of my own. I was afraid to talk to God about my needs because I felt unworthy. Of course, I was unworthy. Still am. Who is worthy of the love of God?

But He doesn't love me because I am worthy of His love. He knows (and I know He knows) all about my weaknesses, but He loves me anyway. I heard it said and I believe it, "For those who believe in God, no explanation is necessary; and for those who don't, no explanation is possible." Far be it from me to attempt an explanation.

I will pose a question: how are self-centered people like us going to become humble? We could go into a discussion here about the id, the ego, the super ego, and all that junk. But we would end up facing the same question, "how?"

Then there's the other question: "Why should I?" Because the defects are part of me, that's why. They are just as much a part of me as my skin, my bones, or any of my vital organs. There are people in the world all around us who have had to undergo surgical amputation of a limb, or the removal of their appendix, gall bladder, tumors, and you name it in order to live. I had to undergo "an amputation" too, in order to live the kind of life I prefer to live, but doctors couldn't do it because they don't know how. Neither did I know how.

I want to remind you, at the risk of boring you with repetition, that we are talking about the exact nature of our wrongs. It will do no good to go to God asking Him to remove our past behavior. What is done is done. When we do something, it becomes history. Even God cannot change it. But He can change us if we're willing to let Him. He can change US so that history does not need to be repeated. You've heard the saying, "If man does not learn from history, he is destined to repeat it." We didn't learn, did we?

Now we can. We'd better. How many vows did I make, how many promises did I break, all the time truly believing that I would really change, only to find myself still as messed up as ever? More so, because each time I made that discovery, I compounded my problem with guilt, remorse, and shame. I would be making promises all over again and trying to invent new lies to cover up the old ones. A squirrel cage going round and round and round. . . .

Humble? Try sincere. Try honest. Sincerely ask Him. Honestly ask Him. Don't go to God and say something like, "Please remove my shortcomings." Good grief! I don't care if you get on your knees, and I don't think God does either, although I have found it to be very effective. But for goodness sake, be sincere. Take some time to talk with God about your character defects. Name them. Ask about each one individually and specifically.

If you're as sick of you as I was of me, you won't find this very hard to do. Those of us who recover do so in part out of desperation.

Remember, three hundred years ago Shakespeare wrote about alcoholism, but he called it "devil." Its nature hasn't changed, only the name it's called by. I was a fool and a beast, were you?

Now for the blockbuster. You are going to God, as I have suggested; you are going to ask that He remove each of your character defects, and He's going to say, "Nope."

Whadda ya mean He's gonna say, "Nope"? You put me through all this stuff, and then you tell me He's gonna say, "Nope"?

Yup.

Whadda ya mean, "yup," He's gonna say "Nope"?

I mean, He ain't a gonna do it.

The apostle Paul had some kind of a character defect. He didn't tell us what it was, and there's been speculation in church groups as to its exact nature. But he just called it a thorn in his side. He said he went to the Lord three times asking to have it removed, and the Lord simply said, "Paul, my grace is sufficient unto you." I went to Him asking to have my character defects removed, and He didn't do it. I'm certainly not any better than Paul, and you're not any better than I am.

But what He will do is help you MANAGE your character defects. They will no longer dictate the terms of your behavior. When they surface, you will control them if you so desire. You have learned, I hope, that what is meant by "our lives had become unmanageable" is that our feelings were out of control. Now you will be able to control them.

I still have every one of my character defects, and sometimes one or two of them will get away from me. But not for long, and that is a tremendous relief for me and a definite benefit to others.

Your character defects were things you were only vaguely aware of and did not understand, so you ignored them. You had to pretend they didn't exist. Others could see them, but you and I were blinded by a drug-affected mind. Now, however, you are aware, and that awareness will set you free. Jesus Christ said, "You will know the truth and the truth will set you free." Remember my young friend who asked if "truth" could be his higher power? More about this awareness in Step Ten.

STEP ONE

We admitted we were powerless over WHATEVER our problem is, that our FEELINGS had become unmanageable.

STEP TWO

Came to believe THAT a power greater than ourselves could restore us to SANITY.

STEP THREE

Made a decision to turn our WANTS and our FEELINGS over to the care of God even though we may not understand Him.

STEP FOUR

Made a searching, SCARY, HONEST inventory of ourselves.

STEP FIVE

Admitted to God, to ourselves and another human being the EXACT nature of our wrongs.

STEP SIX

Were ENTIRELY ready to have God remove ALL these defects of character.

STEP SEVEN

HONESTLY and SINCERELY asked Him to remove our shortcomings.

With an ego like mine you expect humble? Read the step again. I suggested you try sincere or honest. I suggested you talk with God about each character defect—specifically. Let God worry about humble; it may yet come to you.

NOTES

Step Eight

MADE A LIST OF ALL PERSONS WE HAD HARMED AND BECAME WILLING TO MAKE AMENDS TO THEM ALL

If you did a good job on your fourth step, it should be of help to you on this one, because in that step, you would have come across the names of a lot of people you harmed and the ways in which you caused them harm. This step usually raises a lot of questions in people's minds, mostly because they are looking ahead at the next step, "Made direct amends to such people wherever possible except when to do so would injure them or others." I strongly advise you not to look ahead, but just to pay close attention to the job at hand.

It is so easy to start making excuses at this point. This is where the "yah-buts" can interfere and bring about ineffectiveness. The step says ALL PERSONS—all persons we had harmed. It has nothing whatever to do with the fact that someone hurt us, and of course we have been hurt by others. This is not a time to rationalize and justify, but a time of preparation to improve our relationships with others and ourselves.

We have all heard this: "Mommy, he hit me!" "Well, she hit me first!" "That was because he pulled my hair!" "Yah-but d'ya know what she did?" And so on. Now that we are no longer children, it is time to think like adults and time to act like adults and time to accept responsibility for our behavior; past, present, and future. So, just as the step says, we make a list.

It might look something like this:

My parents
My wife/husband
My kids
My boss
My neighbor
My brother
My sister
The judge

The policeman
The school teacher
The grocer
The banker
The taxi driver

If it does, tear it up because it is totally ineffective. I know, because I messed up on this step. I and some others are still paying for my rationalizing. If my mistakes will help someone else, then it's worth sharing. Here's what happened, or I should say did not happen, or a little bit of both or a lot of both, since one way or the other it is no small matter.

My first wife was a nice woman. She was clean, neat, industrious, intelligent, and pretty. We couldn't get along, not because of her, but because of my immaturity, irresponsibility, and all the character defects we have been talking about. She and I had two children, a daughter and a son.

I was not a good husband and I was not a good father. For example, when our little girl was not much more than an infant, I took her and her mother to spend a week with grandma about sixty-five miles away from the little town we were living in. I was to return the next Sunday to bring them home again. On Saturday (payday) when I got off work, I went home and bathed, dressed up and went to the American Legion Club. I had a couple of drinks, put a dime in a slot machine and won ten dollars. A fortune. That would buy a nice gift for my wife as well as a gift for my little girl, wouldn't it? Well, in those days it would have, because my weekly pay was forty dollars. But did it? It went for more drinks and eventually, back into the slot machine along with my entire paycheck. Consequently, I had no money to buy gasoline the next day for the trip to retrieve my family, no money to pay our bills, and no money for groceries so that my family could eat.

One would think that was enough to bring about a decision to stop drinking, but it didn't. My Step One experience didn't happen for another sixteen years or more.

But I was a periodic drunk as opposed to a daily drinker, and the times in between were filled with attempts to be a decent guy. I spent time with my little girl, showered her with attention, and as she grew, had many long talks with her, encouraging and supporting her in the different activities she became involved in, and there were many, because she was a bright and bouncy individual.

My son was also a bright and active little guy, and I tried to be a good dad, even thought that I was. Hoping to help him, I got involved in scouting and in baseball, even though I knew nothing about it, and he and I went on little fishing excursions that were fun. With both of the kids, I became involved in their schools, helped with home work, and was active in the PTA.

Doesn't all this sound like I was a pretty normal dad? Not so.

There were the other times, times of harshness, times when I was too stern, times when I was unkind. They knew that but overlooked it, at least on the surface. There were those times when I drank too much and used family money to do it. But I don't believe they thought much about the money, because somehow there was always enough for their current needs and many of their wants, mainly because their mother also worked and was careful with money. So things were balancing out. My kids were fond of me, especially, I think, my daughter was, I believe because she thought her daddy was just short of perfect.

One night when she was about eleven years old, I came home drunk and attempted to kick the back door in. (Why drunks do some of the things they do will never be known.) The door was not locked; I guess I thought I was John Wayne or some other tough guy. Imagine the noise. You are sitting in your home in the evening, and suddenly someone kicks the door. To say you would be startled is a gross understatement. It would scare the bejabbers out of you.

As I stepped into the house, my little girl came across the room to me, put her arms around my waist and said, "I love you, Daddy." Is that enough to bring about a decision to stop drinking? No. Someone loves you, respects you, looks to you for guidance and protection, expresses that love when you are at your worst; and you continue your love affair with alcohol until that person—son, daughter, wife or whoever—finally can't see anything good about you anymore. You crush the love of a little child, and you hurt that child so deeply that the scars never go away.

More examples we don't need, but there were many. When this girl was about fourteen years old, she saw the sickening truth about her daddy—that he was a liar, a cheater, a womanizer, and thief, to say nothing of a drunkard. She never got over it. They never got over it. My wife, my daughter, and my son. I took their love, respect, and trust and pushed it into their faces.

It was a little different for my son. He was there face-to-face with me when I finally surrendered, and the obsession to drink left me. My daughter was away at college and didn't see what he saw. He saw the miracle; in fact, he was the instrument God used to open the door to a new life. He told me that he saw a physical change take place in me. He was able to trust more completely than his sister that the drinking had come to its end.

When I made a list of all persons I had harmed, I left the names of my wife and kids off that list. Why? Because I rationalized. Me, who no longer had a rational mind. I told myself that yes, I had hurt them, but now that Daddy didn't drink any more, of course they would be delighted. The past would quickly be forgiven and forgotten; therefore it was unnecessary to open the wounds that I was so sure were healing.

Wrong!

I had embarrassed my family. I had shamed my family. I had betrayed my family. The last people on earth to be left off the list of persons we have harmed should be our families, with no excuses, no rationalizing, no yah-buts. If you fail to put them on your list you are going to pay a price. So put them on it.

Your list of persons harmed ought to look something like this:

NAME/WHAT I DID/WHEN/WHAT I CAN DO ABOUT IT
Mom/Stole$25/May 1994 /Pay It Back

The example may be oversimplified, but you get the idea. As in the fourth step, it may be best to use initials instead of names. Also, obviously, this is a private thing that you don't want left lying around. But be specific. I'm aware, too, there are some things you don't want written out so they are legible or intelligible to anyone else, so use a code:

M ST. $ 5/94 PB

or something like that. Otherwise though, write it out!

I have stressed family. All the people you have harmed, whether you were drinking or not, should be listed the same way, along with the specifics of how they were harmed and what you intend to do about it. If you really put your mind to it, and you will if you want to be free and happy, your list is apt to be a long one. Don't leave your own name off the list. You have hurt yourself as much as anyone else.

One last word about this step: you are doing this for YOU, not someone else, although others will undoubtedly benefit. You are doing this so you can hold your head up, no matter where you go. Remember the man in the glass.

STEP ONE

We admitted we were powerless over WHATEVER our problem is, that our FEELINGS had become unmanageable.

STEP TWO

Came to believe THAT a power greater than ourselves could restore us to SANITY.

STEP THREE

Made a decision to turn our WANTS and our FEELINGS over to the care of God even though we may not understand Him.

STEP FOUR

Made a searching, SCARY, HONEST inventory of ourselves.

STEP FIVE

Admitted to God, to ourselves and another human being the EXACT nature of our wrongs.

STEP SIX

Were ENTIRELY ready to have God remove ALL these defects of character.

STEP SEVEN

HONESTLY and SINCERELY asked Him to remove our shortcomings.

STEP EIGHT

Made a list of ALL PERSONS we had harmed and became willing to make amends to them ALL.

PLEASE, PLEASE be careful to include EVERYONE. Do not rationalize, justify, or make excuses for not being absolutely honest. Do not put yourself at risk of paying a very high price for being careless about others' feelings and emotions.

NOTES

Step Nine

MADE DIRECT AMENDS TO SUCH PEOPLE WHEREVER POSSIBLE EXCEPT WHEN TO DO SO WOULD INJURE THEM OR OTHERS

Don't expect the mayor of the city to come forward and declare You Day; don't expect a twenty-one gun salute; don't expect someone or anyone to pin a medal on you; and don't expect people to throw their arms around you and say how wonderful you are just because you stopped drinking, popping pills, snorting whatever, or sniffing something else. After all, you are only doing what every normal person has been doing all along; that is, behaving yourself.

Besides, some people won't believe you, some won't even care, and some never noticed you had a problem to begin with. Those who really care will adopt an attitude of hope with tongue-in-cheek because they've heard your promises before. So I suggest you don't go running around advertising the fact that you have stopped doing whatever it was you were doing. Don't set yourself up for disappointment. Don't expect anything. The rewards will come in time, and they will come in quiet ways, sometimes almost unnoticed.

You are going to make amends, and that isn't easy. I strongly recommend that you be careful, thoughtful, and prayerful as you go about putting your life back in order. I have heard about two sparrows in a bull pen eating manure. After a time one of them flew up and landed on a pitchfork handle. Shortly the other joined it there. The first one flew away and fell dead. The other flew away and it also fell dead. The moral to the story is you should never fly off the handle when you're full of manure.

Direct amends. Direct. adj. straight, without detours; straight forward; candid; blunt; immediate; not turned aside (The New Lexicon Webster's Dictionary Of The English Language). There are, of course, many other definitions of the word, but I have chosen the one that suits our purposes. I'm not so sure about the immediate part. If you have done a good job with Step Eight, you have a task ahead of you that is apt to take a while. If you have not done a good job with Step Eight—go back and do it over, so you don't waste time with this step. But assuming you have done okay up to here, I'm sure you realize you have a lot of people to see.

Amends. sing. and pl. n. to make compensation, reparation or restitution (for loss or injury). (Same dictionary). But that same dictionary also says: to correct; free from faults; to change for the better. My own definition is more satisfactory to me: Amend. v. fix. After all, you can look at it as two words, can't you? "A mend." Something is broken or torn or damaged, so you fix it. Some of the things we've done to others are going to take some effort on our part to mend. I say to you, some of the things we have done cannot be fixed directly, but we can go into that a bit later.

Some of the damage that took us but a few seconds to create may take a lifetime to correct. Jesus Christ said, "But I say unto you, that whosoever is angry with his brother without a cause shall be in danger of the judgment, and whosoever shall say to his brother, Raca, shall be in danger of the council; but whosoever shall say, Thou fool, shall be in danger of hell fire." (the Holy Bible, King James Version)

Have you ever called someone a fool? Have you ever said, "Go to hell!" to anyone? How long does that take? Try it. See how many times you can say, "go to hell!" in one minute. The damage is perhaps permanent. Some folks are touchy, you know; they don't like to be talked down to.

Some folks are vengeful, carry grudges so long that they begin to like it, and won't want to let go of their resentments when you come to them, more especially if you aren't sincere. Almost anyone can spot a phony. So don't go to people unless you truly have become willing to make amends. Even then, you might meet one or two who will not accept what you have to say. But for the most part, you will find people will not reject you.

If you go with humility and honesty and tell the person what it is you are trying to do, that is, rebuild your life; if you go with facts as to how you have harmed them; if you go with a definite plan of restitution, you will probably find people are interested and caring enough to hear you out and to offer encouragement and support. It would also be a good idea to pray before you go, asking God's direction in what you plan to do. That's optional. It is what I would do. Refer to Step Three.

Some that you need to approach have moved away. I was told by a friend that he received a letter from another state from a person he hadn't seen in a very long time—so long that he had forgotten there was such a person, someone he had not known very well at that. The letter informed him that the man was attempting to rebuild his life, and he had learned that to do so successfully he needed to follow the step we are discussing here. He told my friend that when they were in high school, they had adjoining lockers and that he had stolen two dollars from my friend's locker. He apologized, enclosed the two dollars and asked forgiveness. Not only was he forgiven, but they became very good friends. Obviously, the man had done some research to find out where my friend was at the time. What he had no way of knowing was that my friend was using this very same program and understood perfectly where the man was coming from. You never know what good things can come from trying to do the right thing.

You may not be able to find everyone. Furthermore, the step has a built-in loophole. "Made direct amends to such people wherever possible." In some cases that lets you off the hook, does it not? Yes, it does not! (Thirteen big, black bugs in a basket. Lovely thought, is it not? Yes, it is not!) Indirect amends can always be made. Always. Why do you want off the hook anyway? You're doing this for you. Don't cheat yourself. Keep looking for the rewards. Keep working for the peace of mind that can and will come when you have done your best to right the wrongs.

A man came to me once with a troublesome problem. He was trying to make amends but ran into a situation he just didn't know how to handle. He told me this story from his past: He had been living for several years in a small upstairs apartment, across the hall from another man who had been there several years also.

One afternoon his landlady came to his door very distressed because the man across the hall from him had died. He went with her to investigate. Upon finding out it was true, he told her to go downstairs and telephone the authorities, and he would stay with the body. While she was gone, he happened to glance around the room. His eyes fell on a coffee can on the floor just inside the open closet door.

His first mistake was to look in the can. His second was to take the rather large sum of money he found there. The dead man, he knew, had no known living relatives. So the whole thing caught up with him when he began to put his life back in order. He had very little money of his own at the time he came to me. He was afraid of the authorities, and he didn't know what to do.

I suggested that he examine his income and his expenses, make a decision as to how much he could pay per week, and come back to see me. He did just that. When he returned and told me how much he could pay, I suggested that he add five dollars to that amount and give that total to a church or some charity every week until he was satisfied that he had made restitution. To the best of my knowledge he has done so, but I haven't seen him for many years now.

The step says, "Made direct amends to such people wherever possible . . . " leaving me to believe that "indirect" is intended where direct amends cannot be made. More on this a little further on.

The step continues, " . . . except when to do so would injure them or others." The man in the story above could, I suppose, have gone to the authorities, made a clean breast of the affair, and faced the music. But this man had an invalid sister and an aged mother who were dependent upon him both basically and emotionally. Direct amends could not have been made to the dead man, and direct amends to society would have injured innocent people: his mother and sister. So indirect amends were suggested.

Suppose you've had an affair outside your marriage. Your spouse does not know. If the other party was married, his or her spouse does not know. You do not, under any circumstances, go to these people and try to make amends. To do so will only cause life-long problems for all four of you. There are alternatives to direct amends.

I'm certain that you will know of other circumstances in which direct amends are either impossible or totally unrealistic, and indirect amends seem to be as well. Someone will say, "My father is dead. How do I make amends to him?" Write a letter to him, explaining what you have done to harm him, what you wish you could do about it, and what you intend to do about it. Now what did I mean by that? You've just told me your father is dead, and I tell you to write a letter to him and then even tell him in that letter what you intend to do about the harm you've caused. I should hope that what you intend to do about it is to be the very best person you can be from here on out and honor the memory of your father or anyone else to whom direct amends are impossible. Destroy the letter when you have finished it and put your past life behind you.

I can never make amends to my family by giving back the time stolen from them, by undoing the embarrassment and shame I caused them, or by taking back the verbal abuse they suffered. There are others I harmed, some seriously, that I do not have a way of finding and could not make amends for the harm if I did find them. The only thing I can do is to live my life in such a way as to show them that I love them and realize the harm I have caused. I can make amends by being a sober, honest, worthwhile person, practicing love and respect for others, whoever or wherever they are. I can make a decision each day to make someone's life a little better, even if all I have to offer is a smile. I can be clean, sober, and perhaps a good influence on someone, somewhere.

Have you ever walked past a flower garden, stopping momentarily to take in the beauty? As you continue on your way, your life is a little better because of the flowers. But the flowers don't know that they have influenced you. Too, so do you and I influence those who pass through our lives, for good or bad. If it is for good, then we are making indirect amends for our past.

As long as we're on this earth, we'll continue to have problems. If we learn to pay attention to ourselves, we can avoid problems developing into trouble. Step Ten is a tool that will help us with self-awareness.

STEP ONE

We admitted we were powerless over WHATEVER our problem is, that our FEELINGS had become unmanageable.

STEP TWO

Came to believe THAT a power greater than ourselves could restore us to SANITY.

STEP THREE

Made a decision to turn our WANTS and our FEELINGS over to the care of God even though we may not understand Him.

STEP FOUR

Made a searching, SCARY, HONEST inventory of ourselves.

STEP FIVE

Admitted to God, to ourselves and another human being the EXACT nature of our wrongs.

STEP SIX

Were ENTIRELY ready to have God remove ALL these defects of character.

STEP SEVEN

HONESTLY and SINCERELY asked Him to remove our shortcomings.

STEP EIGHT

Made a list of ALL persons we had harmed and became willing to make amends to them ALL.

STEP NINE

Made DIRECT amends to such people WHEREVER POSSIBLE except when to do so would injure them or others. (Otherwise we made INDIRECT amends.)

It isn't always possible for various reasons to make DIRECT amends but there are always ways to make INDIRECT amends.

Very seldom will your direct amends be rejected—people are usually glad you are making a change. So, although it is a scary thing to do, it is in your own best interests to go directly to people. When this is impossible, find ways to make indirect amends. Free your own conscience.

NOTES

Step Ten

CONTINUED TO TAKE PERSONAL INVENTORY AND WHEN WE WERE WRONG PROMPTLY ADMITTED IT

And they lived happily ever after—the end sentence in how many fairy tales, I don't know, but a lot of them. But this is no fairy tale. This is reality, and it's true that you can live happily ever after, even though there are bound to be unhappy events in your life from time to time. Remember Abraham Lincoln said, "People are about as happy as they make up their minds to be," and I believe we can be happy even when things are not going the way we want them to, if we are at peace with ourselves and, as far as humanly possible, at peace with the world.

A number of different attitudes can influence our successful use of this step, and we choose the attitudes we want to live by. A friend of mine used to say, "If you sober up a drunken horse thief, you then have a sober horse thief." In other words, not drinking is not enough. True sobriety brings about change in attitude, change in thought, and change in behavior. These changes can and do bring about true happiness, serenity and peace of mind. When we have achieved this state, the urge to drink, overeat, pop up, shoot up, or whatever else it is we are trying to overcome, is gone and will stay gone, so long as we continue with our self-examination and promptly admit it when we are wrong.

There have been times, when I was talking with people who are using these steps to better their lives, someone told me they believed it was time for them to "take another fifth step." My usual response to this remark is, "Why?" Invariably, I am told they believe they "missed something" they have done in the past or that they "now remember" something they have done that they didn't talk about in Step Five.

I like to ask such persons what approach they used to the fourth step. Then I remind them that we do not take inventory of what we have done, rather we take inventory of what caused us to do it. If they used examples of all the causes, then they did not miss anything in Step Five. I then point out the reason for Step Ten is so that we need not repeat Steps Four and Five. It is important to remember Step Five is not a confessional, but a self-evaluation, and Step Ten is a continuation of that process, making it a way of life.

However, and this is important, it may be that what you have remembered requires you to add someone to your list in Step Eight and then make the amends called for in Step Nine. Otherwise, continue with Step Ten to prevent future trouble with your relationships.

Steps Ten, Eleven, and Twelve have been referred to as “the Maintenance Steps,” and with good reason. They are the steps that help us continue a new way of living that keeps us in harmony with ourselves, others, and our Creator. It is by virtue of these steps that we continue to learn, grow and develop into the kind of happy, peaceful, productive people we have always yearned to be.

So, Step Ten, “ . . . continued . . . ” The word is self-explanatory, and it implies action of some sort, in this case action of the mental kind. The dictionary puts it this way: “to go on with (an action).”

Of course, there are different ways to approach this step. I have heard of several. For example, I have seen a card printed somewhat like a score card for miniature golf. Apparently, it is the purpose of this card to assist us in our effort to continue to take personal inventory. It looks something like this:

LIABILITIES									ASSETS
	SUN	MON	TUE	WED	THUR	FRI	SAT	SUN	
PRIDE									FAITH
SELFISHNESS									HOPE
IMPATIENCE									CHARITY
DISHONEST THINKING									COURTESY
ETC.									KINDNESS
ETC.									LOYALTY
ETC.									PATIENCE

and more etceteras, with lines in between vertically and horizontally to make nice little squares which are to be used for check marks as we sit at the end of our week and look ourselves over, to see what we may have done wrong and where we need to make amends. Or I guess the thing can be rigged so that we sit at the end of our day and decide where we have been wrong and what things need to be mended.

But the step does not work that way. It was never meant to work that way. If you try to make it work that way, you are in for disappointment. You're going to be wondering why things don't seem better than they used to be, or if you're not wondering, someone else will be.

Supposedly you have become aware of your personality defects and your assets. This awareness is meant to help you in life, to make things better for yourself and those around you. You have discovered the tools of living, and you need to stop putting off their use even for a day. Look at that sentence. "Supposedly" you have become aware. This is the key to better living, to kindness, to courtesy, to honesty, to patience, and to all the other character assets that are a part of you and the key to your own peace of mind.

Let's play a little game of old-time cowboys for a minute. Picture yourself as a wild, rough, hard-drinking leader of a scroungy bunch of horse thieves. If you're a woman, you're probably thinking, "Well, that leaves me out." Don't. What do you think Ma Barker was, a society deb? Come on, just get in the saddle with the rest of us. But something happens along the trail somewhere and you give it all up, turn your back on the gang, and ride off through the hills with a new resolve to live a sober, clean, productive life.

Here you are, riding a beautiful, powerful horse through a beautiful part of the country with rolling hills, green grass, and plenty of good clean water, and you're feeling very good about yourself for the first time in many years. Quite suddenly, after two days of travel, you crest a knoll and there below you is a herd of horses. There is no one around, and you have seen no sign of anyone the last two days.

Changing a way of life is not easy. Have we sobered up a drunken horse thief only to find a sober horse thief? So easy it would be to cut out a half dozen or so and drive them somewhere to sell them. Well, maybe just a couple of them, like that little mare and her colt over on the south side. "I'm a-gonna need some cash to help me start this here new way of life I've been a-thinkin' about when I git to some town. I reckon I'll just take 'em two along, sorta borry 'em like." This guy can clearly see his character defects and decides not to let them dictate his behavior.

"Whoooa, there pard! Thet'd be wrong. Thet there is my old way a-thinkin' 'n it's jest the sorta thing I'm a-tryin' ta git away from 'n' I ain't a-gonna do it." And you ride on through the hills "feelin' a mite better" about yourself.

THAT is Step Ten. Our horse thief knew nothing about Step Ten, but he knew a great deal about his own dishonesty. You should

Wrong page 96 2nd paragraph says + make ammends still neglected!

notice in our little story, there is no one around but the "reformed" thief. When he was wrong, he promptly admitted it to HIMSELF. Promptly. BEFORE he committed the act. You see, in Steps Ten, Eleven, and Twelve there is nothing said about making amends. Making amends is strictly Step Nine. But Step Ten, properly used, makes Step Nine unnecessary, because we admit we are wrong before we commit whatever action we are about to take.

What I'm suggesting is that you pay attention to your thoughts and feelings all the time, because therein lie your character defects as well as your character assets. Defects and assets of the personality are the motivators of our thoughts, and our thoughts are the motivators of our behavior. If our thoughts are about being honest, if they are about caring for others and doing the right thing, then we are pretty apt to be satisfied with ourselves without the aid of artificial stimulation, such as eating too much, drinking, using other drugs, going on spending sprees, or losing the farm at a game we never should have been playing in the first place.

There is yet another aspect of continuing to take personal inventory. It seems to me that a personal inventory should involve the person who is taking the inventory. We have been discussing ways to improve your relationships with others. Remember there is also a "you" involved here, and you should never lose sight of that. Are you taking care of you? Are you changing for the betterment of yourself? How often we hear it said that old habits die hard. For that reason, it is a good idea for you to take a very close look at your habits and to know which are good for you and which are harmful.

You have a physical self, an emotional self and a mental self that need your attention. I am willing to bet that for a long time, you have neglected you to the point of developing habits that are unhealthy on all three counts. For happiness, serenity and peace of mind, these will need to be changed and new habits developed. A big help in that direction will be to pay attention to yourself by using a moment-to-moment inventory. Where there is dirt, let there be soap and water; where there is hunger, let there be regular meals; where there is fatigue, let there be regular rest and sleep; where there is profanity, let there be intelligent speech (I heard a proverb somewhere that says: "If a man's thoughts are not wiser than the wind, it is well if he remains silent and listens to the wind."); where there is stress, let there be communication, recreation, prayer, and meditation.

That is what the next step is all about.

STEP ONE

We admitted we were powerless over WHATEVER our problem is, that our FEELINGS had become unmanageable.

STEP TWO

Came to believe THAT a power greater than ourselves could restore us to SANITY.

STEP THREE

Made a decision to turn our WANTS and our FEELINGS over to the care of God even though we may not understand Him.

STEP FOUR

Made a searching, SCARY, HONEST inventory of ourselves.

STEP FIVE

Admitted to God, to ourselves and another human being the EXACT nature of our wrongs.

STEP SIX

Were ENTIRELY ready to have God remove ALL these defects of character.

STEP SEVEN

HONESTLY and SINCERELY asked Him to remove our shortcomings.

STEP EIGHT

Made a list of ALL persons we had harmed and became willing to make amends to them ALL.

STEP NINE

Made DIRECT amends to such people wherever possible except when to do so would injure them or others. (Otherwise we made INDIRECT amends.)

STEP TEN

Continued to take a MOMENT-TO-MOMENT personal inventory and when we were wrong PROMPTLY admitted it.

To maintain happiness, serenity and peace of mind, a big help will be to take a moment-to-moment inventory, paying attention to your thoughts and feelings, asking yourself, "Am I about to do the right thing or is this wrong?" If it's wrong, admit it RIGHT AWAY and don't act on it.

If you live this way you will seldom (though sometimes) need Step Nine.

NOTES

Step Eleven

SOUGHT THROUGH PRAYER AND MEDITATION TO IMPROVE OUR CONSCIOUS CONTACT WITH GOD AS WE UNDERSTOOD HIM—PRAYING ONLY FOR KNOWLEDGE OF HIS WILL FOR US AND THE POWER TO CARRY THAT OUT

I believe in miracles. I am one. I am a walking, talking miracle. I like being what I am, who I am, and what I believe in and stand for. That doesn't mean there is no room for improvement, it only means I know I am a much better person than I once was. And it feels good inside, like warm fuzzies where there used to be cold pricklies.

What have I done to change? Nothing at all without a whole lot of help. Some of that help, the major part of it, came directly from God in terms of my being set free from my obsession to drink. The rest of it came from God working through people who, in spite of my unworthiness, or perhaps because of it, loved me enough to teach and teach and teach this way of life until it all began to sink in. I have "lived happily ever after." But they couldn't have helped if I had not had a willing heart, and the willing heart came as a gift from God.

So everything about me is a miraculous gift for which I can never find a way to express my gratitude to God Himself and to the people He sent to help me, and there have been many.

I was in Amarillo, Texas and so near broke I was afraid to spend anything. However, in a little book store, I found a small booklet of "Inspirational Verse" priced at thirty-five cents. So I treated myself. A verse I discovered in that little booklet may be appropriate to express how I feel toward all those who cared enough to try to help me, even when I did not respond:

"I love you. Not only for what you are
but for what you are making of yourself.
I love you not only for what you are
but for what I am when I'm with you.

I love you for putting your hand into my heaped up heart
And passing over all the weak and foolish things
you can't help dimly seeing there
And bringing out into the light all the beautiful
belongings no one else looked deep enough to find.

I love you for helping me build of the timber
of my life not a tavern, but a temple
And of the works of my every day
Not a reproach, but a song."

—Anonymous

I guess we could say I'm a fundamentalist as far as the Bible goes. I believe every word in the Bible is the truth, and I refuse to be dissuaded by the arguments of scholars, theologians, religious groups, scientists, or anyone who wishes to argue. If the Bible says it, I believe it, and that settles it. And what the Bible says about prayer is, "Rejoice evermore. Pray without ceasing. In everything give thanks for this is the will of God through Christ Jesus concerning you."

But I'll tell you the truth; I have not learned to pray without ceasing. Someone once said that prayer is when we talk to God and meditation is when He talks to us. That makes sense to me, but how does one talk to God? I used a poem I had learned as my prayer. It was a very high-minded sort of poem that was beyond what should have been reasonable expectation, but I didn't know a better way. As a result—there was no result. I prayed to be made a man of strength and character, and became a drunkard.

Earlier I mentioned prayer versus yarping. If you look at the word pray, it could be broken down as follows: p=praise; r=repent; a=ask for others; y=yourself. In other words, being thankful, being sorry for wrong doing, caring for others, and caring for self. Yarping is just the opposite, which of course puts our selves ahead of everyone, including God.

Does God answer prayer? Of course He does, when He can. Look at the Bible quote above. In EVERYTHING give thanks. Even for a broken leg? Yes. God dwells in the praises of His people. He cannot live in complaints, therefore when we complain in our prayers, God cannot help us, even though He wants to.

I heard a story about a man who was depressed and bitter. Life hadn't treated him the way he had hoped, so he decided to end it all. He went down to the sea shore to drown himself. As he began to walk out into the water, he thought that this being his last chance, he would do himself some good if he talked with God. So he began his usual complaining, telling God how bad everything was and why he had decided on suicide. Even as he asked God to make th better, he continued to walk deeper into the water. To make things worse, a flock of birds flew overhead and one made a "splat" right on his head. "You see, God," he said, "for other people they sing."

If we thank God for all things that happen to us, He will make bad things better, because He can act on positive situations. If we complain, He can't help because He cannot act on negative thoughts, feelings, and actions. He doesn't live in the negative, He lives in the positive, and that means in praise. I refer you to "Power in Praise", a book written by Merlin Carrothers. He explains all this better than I can.

Meanwhile, talk to God as you would to anyone else (see Step Three of this book); keep it simple. As you go through your day from beginning to end, develop the habit of saying "Thank you God" every time something happens, good or bad. You don't have to say it out loud. He knows your thoughts. In fact, I recommend you don't say it out loud, because the world would certainly not understand. However, I think there are times in the day when it is appropriate to verbalize our gratitude. Don't be ashamed of being grateful, and certainly don't be ashamed of believing in God.

I also believe that our lives can be a prayer. If we keep ourselves clean and neat, if we clean up our language, put a smile on our faces, try to help others, and in general live the way God wants us to live, loving Him and loving His, then I believe that is a prayer in itself. It is a message to God saying, "I agree with you and I'm trying to show it."

Meditation—I can lay no claim to being a thinker. When I try to meditate by thinking, my thoughts scatter all over creation, refusing to stay on one subject for more than a few seconds at a time, day dreaming, wishing, reminiscing, or as some people have called it, chasing rainbows (and I never catch any). By thinking meditatively, I seldom accomplish much.

In a group setting once, it was suggested by our group facilitator that we find a nice quiet, comfortable, relaxing spot and sit quietly for ten minutes with our eyes closed. The day was a warm, sunny, October day; one of those when we really appreciate life. I found a place where I sat in the grass with my back against a brick wall, where silence ruled except for the quiet bird songs nearby, closed my eyes, breathed deeply, and relaxed. What a nice time in my life that was. I will remember it always. Time drifted by and peace reigned. When I finally opened my eyes, two minutes had elapsed. Not ten but two. That kind of meditating doesn't work well for me either.

For a short while years ago, I had a roommate who practiced Yoga or something. He never told me what he was practicing, but if I made the slightest noise, he would tell me loud and clear that he was meditating. I had wondered what it was that he was doing; he sat on his pillow at the end of his bed with his right leg tied to his left leg by its foot, and his left leg tied to his right leg by its foot, and his two arms twisted around each other as if some huge wrestler had accosted him, then gone away and left him in that condition. I didn't ask him, but I wondered if he might be meditating on the best way to extricate himself from the situation he found himself in. I also wondered if I ought to call for help, but I didn't. When I saw him later, walking down the hallway, I decided he had found the answer to his puzzle by himself.

Of all the methods of meditation I have heard of, the one that works best for me is to read. Reading directs my mind, and keeps it on track so that I can follow the subject of my meditation. In this case, the subject of my meditation is God, and I find no better way to think about Him and to communicate with Him than to read the Bible.

People have said, "I don't understand the Bible." Have you read it? Others have said, "The Bible contradicts itself." No, it does not. Have you read it, or have you only poked around in there a little bit? If the King James version gives you trouble, buy a modern translation. I don't claim to understand all of the Bible, but I understand that which is important to me, namely God's will for me. His will and my will are the same thing. Hold on a minute, that is about to be explained.

Think of it this way: you have a very rich relative, and you have good reason to believe that relative loves you. Your relative dies and leaves a will. Do you want to know what is in that will? If your own will is what you want, as we discussed in Step Three, isn't God's will what He wants? Is God rich? The Bible says the earth is the Lord's and the fullness thereof. How rich can you get? Is God your father? He left a will, and that will is in the Bible. Well, whether you read it or not, I will continue to read it, as opposed to sitting around waiting for a voice to come booming out of heaven. And besides, in reading the Bible, I have already learned what God wants for me, and I am certain it is the same as He wants for you.

The Bible says that the sole duty of man is to love God. So from that, I know what He wants from me. You can elaborate on that universally, because to love God it is necessary to love everything He created. Even your mother-in-law—unconditionally. The Bible also says, "Dearly beloved, I would above all else that you prosper and be in health."

So from that, I know what God wants for me. Isn't prosperity and good health exactly what you want for yourself? It is certainly what I want for me, and that is why I said above that His will and my will are the same thing. The only difference is that He knows how to get it for me, and I don't.

So we pray for "the power to carry that out." The Bible says, "Whatsoever you find for your hand to do, do it with your might." I have become convinced that if we do our best with what we are called on to do, God will turn it to a blessing. I was given an early example of that when I was in the army, but I'm sad to say the message never came through until many years later, probably because I was already pretty deeply involved in alcohol. I was not on the best of terms with the first field sergeant, and it seemed that when some menial detail came along I was the first one he thought of, but I was not the only one.

One day the sergeant called a dozen of us together and led us to the mess hall where we were told to carry the tables outside. Each of us was provided with a rag, a bucket of water, and a bayonet. Our duty was to soak the table with water from the bucket and scrape it down with the bayonet until the very top level of the wood had been removed, thus "cleaning" the tables. We worked in pairs. The fellow who worked with me was a lad with a cheerful attitude, and we really tried to do a good job, joking with each other all the while about the "fact" that the army was unaware of what a pair of talented young men we were, and that one of these days we would be "discovered." Meanwhile, the others in the detail grumbled, complained, and put forth little effort.

The next day, the sergeant called his favorites together for some more of the same detail. We were marched to the mess hall and told to repeat the process of the day before. But then the mess sergeant came on the scene and told the first field sergeant that the two of us had done a good job, and done it cheerfully at that. He said that in no way were we to join in the detail again, and he was prepared to make that an order. We were excused from the detail.

Guess what? Two weeks later I found myself transferred to division headquarters, where I had a class A job, a class A uniform, and a class A pass. I never again worked on a meaningless detail and soon had a few stripes of my own. One day while out on my class A pass, I heard my name and, turning around, came face to face with my partner of the bayonet squad with his class A uniform, class A pass, and a class A job in corps headquarters. I'm not going to say God rewarded us for cleaning mess tables, but I'm not sure He didn't reward us for having a cheerful attitude while we did it.

Maybe even a smile can be a prayer. My mother, who is ninety-seven years old, currently lives in a nursing home, where I go to visit her every other day as near as I can. A nursing home can be a pretty depressing place no matter how hard the staff try to liven it up. Often I will see someone sitting in a wheelchair with a bland look on their face, until I smile at them and speak so that they know the smile is meant for them. It is like seeing the sun come from behind a cloud when their faces light up. A smile, a cheery word, a touch of the hand; these are the things that God is made of, and that He wants us to share with others.

And sharing is a lot of what the next step is about.

Since I wrote the above, my mother has died. She was a person with a wonderful sense of humor. One of her favorite things was a stuffed animal called "Beeples." Beeples was so named because he beeped with a rapid giggling sound when he was turned so that light hit his eyes, and his nose flashed a yellow light. Mother died with Beeples in her arms, his face snuggled to her chest. When the undertaker came for her body, he just took Beeples along. That same Sunday afternoon, as the undertaker, in the building alone, was ready to begin preparation of Mother's body, he picked up Beeples and exposed his face to the light. In telling me of it afterward, the man said, "He scared the hell out of me! He talks back!" I am absolutely convinced that Mother was laughing, her sense of humor still intact. And I believe her smile was a prayer.

STEP ONE

We admitted we were powerless over WHATEVER our problem is, that our FEELINGS had become unmanageable.

STEP TWO

Came to believe THAT a power greater than ourselves could restore us to SANITY.

STEP THREE

Made a decision to turn our WANTS and our FEELINGS over to the care of God even though we may not understand Him.

STEP FOUR

Made a searching, SCARY, HONEST inventory of ourselves.

STEP FIVE

Admitted to God, to ourselves and to another human being the EXACT nature of our wrongs.

STEP SIX

Were ENTIRELY ready to have God remove ALL these defects of character.

STEP SEVEN

HONESTLY and SINCERELY asked Him to remove our shortcomings.

STEP EIGHT

Made a list of ALL PERSONS we had harmed and became willing to make amends to them ALL.

STEP NINE

Made DIRECT amends to such persons wherever possible except when to do so would injure them or others. (Otherwise, we made INDIRECT amends.)

STEP TEN

Continued to take a MOMENT TO MOMENT personal inventory and when we were wrong PROMPTLY admitted it.

STEP ELEVEN

Sought through prayer and meditation to improve our conscious contact with God even though we may not understand Him, praying, NOT YARPING only for knowledge of His will for us and the power to carry that out.

NOTES

Step Twelve

HAVING HAD A SPIRITUAL AWAKENING AS A RESULT OF THESE STEPS, WE TRIED TO CARRY THIS MESSAGE TO ALCOHOLICS AND TO PRACTICE THESE PRINCIPLES IN ALL OUR AFFAIRS

> It is one of the most beautiful compensations of life that no man can sincerely try to help another without helping himself.
>
> –Ralph Waldo Emerson

I believe in the resurrection because my spirit was not just asleep, it was dead. Now it is not only alive, but it is awake, and that is another miracle. I did not just say to my spirit one morning that it was time to wake up and get going. I didn't even know my spirit, much less know how to awaken it. I had another spirit, though. It was not a very nice one, not one that you would care to know and not one that I care to have anything to do with again. I hold it responsible for the nasty, hurtful things I did. When my son confronted me that night so long ago, it died. Good riddance.

Everyone has the potential for goodness, for happiness, serenity and peace of mind, for a belly full of warm fuzzies. Everyone. But these qualities may be asleep. Or dead. They can be resurrected, but not just at the snap of the fingers. Not just because we stop using whatever artificial means we were using to create what we thought were those characteristics. They need to be recognized in their infancy, nourished and trained; that is what these Twelve Steps help us to accomplish.

I don't like alarm clocks, and I don't like rude awakenings. I much prefer to be awakened quietly and gently. I don't wake up quickly either. I don't jump from my bed and start singing. Rather, I head directly to the coffee pot, fill my cup and sit at the table hanging on to that cup for dear life lest I fall off my chair. I want the light to be dim, and voices quiet at least for the first half-hour.

At first, my recovery came about the same way. I was hanging on for dear life. The light was dim, the voices quiet and distant. But by using the steps, I gradually became aware of myself, eventually became aware of others and finally became aware of the presence of God in my life as a Power that could and would help me, not just in times of trouble and stress, but at all times. Thus came about the awakening of my spirit.

I see the twelfth step in two parts. Part one, a spiritual awakening, has occurred as a result of using the first eleven steps, so the awakening is not really a part of the twelfth step. That leaves part two, a message to carry and principles to practice.

It is a natural inclination when we begin our recovery process to want to help others, because we feel so much better about ourselves. It feels as if we have overcome our addiction, and the shame, remorse, fear, and anxiety have been greatly relieved. So it is not surprising when someone who has just begun to use this program goes out to save the world. They have recognized Step One, begun to feel the results of freedom, had a dim glimpse of Step Twelve and off they go. Perhaps they do as much harm as good. Their message is incomplete, and others cannot relate. That's why there are twelve steps instead of two. Simple.

I was fortunate enough to have a man named Pepper as a sponsor to lead, teach and show me the right things to do and say for the first few years of my recovery. The very first thing I want to share with you about helping others is that when someone calls and tells you they want help, do not go alone. You never know what you may be walking into; I assure you, we walked into some very bad situations. Do not go alone. Don't go at all if you're not dead serious. Remember, this very well could mean the difference between life and death to someone.

Pepper was no stranger to desolation. He was well acquainted with loneliness and fear and guilt. It had been said of him that there was not a bar in the state where someone had not stepped over him lying on the floor and said, "Poor Pepper." He told me numerous times that "Poor Pepper" was the last thing he needed, but the thing he craved the most in his drunken state. He understood alcoholism. He understood the alcoholic. He cared. Deeply. But his feelings were not sympathy, they were empathy. He had an ability to see and express the needs of others in more than words. He believed in doing.

I often think of a time when he and I had been called to the local hotel by the management. They were concerned about a resident who had been locked in his room for several days, repeatedly ordering whiskey by the fifth from room service and not venturing from his room to the dining room or anywhere else, to their knowledge.

Armed with this much information and a pass key, we went up to the room.

Pepper opened the door, and we both staggered back several steps from the stench that poured out into the hall. We stepped in and turned on the light. I can never forget what we found and what followed. A heavy green blind was pulled over the window, which was closed. The room was littered with bottles and vomit. On the bed lay a man so thin one almost had to look twice to see him there (a slight exaggeration on my part of course).

Pepper said, "Oh, my god! Go get a bottle of booze, a bottle of orange juice and a jar of honey. Quick!" When I returned a few minutes later, the window shade was up, the window was open, the empty bottles (eighteen of them, as it turned out) were stacked in a corner, and Pepper was on his hands and knees cleaning up the man's vomit. Pepper cared.

In those days, hospitals would deny admission to a drunk. We really can't blame them. Drunks are loud, belligerent, obnoxious and, at times, dangerous. Consider the possibility that little old Mrs. Whatzername has a bad heart, is being treated for a recent attack, needs quiet and rest, and here comes John Hasaloadon, singing at the top of his lungs and bumping into everything in his path; he strolls into her room and says, "Well, hi there! Whazza matter with you?"

John doesn't know he's messing up; he may not even know where he is. I've heard it said that alcoholics are like Columbus. Columbus didn't know where he was going, when he got there he didn't know where he was, when he got back he didn't know where he'd been, and he did it all with money he borrowed from some dame. So it was natural that hospitals were very careful about drunks.

So we learned to take care of them ourselves in the best way we knew how. What does a drunk want? Another drink. So we would give them one. I suppose you could call it a cocktail of sorts, being three-fourths whiskey or vodka, or whatever we had, and one-fourth honey and orange juice. As we continued the detoxification process, we increased the honey and orange juice and decreased the booze accordingly, until the person was off the liquor entirely, drinking and eating nourishing food. We were trying to avoid having our "patient" go into D.T.'s. It nearly always worked, but it sometimes took three days and nights. Even then, we were afraid the danger wasn't past.

That is the "treatment" we gave the man in the hotel. In a few days, he was on his feet and then disappeared. We never saw him again or heard from him, so we don't know how it turned out for him. But there were others, cases perhaps not as severe, with whom we were successful. If they stayed around and tried, we could then share our own stories with them. We saw some lives change. Not always, but one person saved in a lifetime is worth more than anything I can think of.

Pepper taught me to go the limit, and he taught me what that means. Calling on someone in need isn't always convenient. It is seldom pleasant. But it surely is rewarding when the program works for someone and you witness lives coming back together, families reunited, and health and happiness restored. On one occasion, the hospital called me to visit a patient for whom they expressed concern that a drinking problem was ruining his health. With this one, I found I had to go the limit.

It was obvious from the start that the man was interested in what I had to say, realized he was in serious trouble with alcohol, and wanted to stop. In the next couple of weeks, he tried but relapsed and then couldn't stop again. After several attempts followed by relapses, it was decided he needed more than we could give him. The message wasn't getting through because he couldn't stay dry long enough to clear his head. We made arrangements to send him to a treatment center in another state.

On a windy, cold, snowy day I was driving him the 120 miles to the airport for his flight to treatment, when out in the middle of nowhere the fan belt on my car broke. We missed the flight. So we made all the arrangements over again, and the next time I picked him up to make the trip to the airport, he was drunk. At the gate, the flight attendant stopped him, because his condition was obvious, and said, "Sir, I believe you are drunk; I'm sorry, but I can't let you board the aircraft." Probably for the same reasons hospitals were so careful.

Anyway, the attendant wasn't going to let our man aboard. Without hesitation, I stepped forward, put on my sternest expression, turned on the most professional voice I could come up with on the spur of the moment, and told the attendant that I was Dr. so and so, this man's physician, that the man had a very serious health problem and that it was absolutely imperative that he arrive at his destination, a matter of life and death. As we all know, people think doctors are God's personal representatives, and the attendant was no exception. His response was something like, "Oh, yes, doctor, as long as you vouch for him, he can board. We'll see to his comfort as much as possible."

When my "patient" was on that plane, I headed for my car. When those wheels left the ground I was, as they say, "out of there." I don't recommend anyone trying this in these times. Things have changed at airports and, if you'll excuse a pun, it wouldn't fly.

That is one example of what I mean by 'go the limit'. We would lie, impersonate or whatever it took to help someone get a chance at recovery, because "but for the grace of God, there go I."

I have always been grateful to that airline attendant. He, too, went the limit, broke the rules, cast aside caution, and became one of life's unsung heroes. And he doesn't even know it—an example of God working through people. Shortly after my friend's arrival at the treatment facility, his heart stopped. He was only revived because there were nurses right on the spot. He came home a month later sober, happy, and grinning ear to ear. His family was delighted, and so were the rest of us. The last I knew of him, about a year and a half later, he was still grinning.

I received a call one afternoon from a man who said he needed help, that he was desperate and he sure sounded as if he were. He was about five minutes drive away. Though there was no one available at the time to go with me, I drove over to his house. There was no answer at the door when I knocked, so I went around the house to the back, walked onto a screened-in porch and knocked on a partially open door. Again no answer. I pushed the door open and stepped into a kitchen with blood all over the floor. The man had cut his wrist. I was able to get him hospitalized, and he came out of it okay—that time.

Shortly thereafter, I moved to another town. About a year later, I read an account in a newspaper of that same man barricading himself and his girlfriend in his house and having a shoot-out with the police. He shot and killed his girlfriend and himself. They don't all have happy endings. But the people you're called on to help won't necessarily be in such bad straits.

Hospitals have changed their attitudes. Most have made arrangements for a " detox unit" where the addicted person is treated with medication, if not a certain amount of respect.

It may be that all you need to do for and with the person who asks for your help is to tell your story and share your knowledge of these steps and how to best use them.

If that is so, and I pray it is, make sure the person is willing to listen to you, then tell your story. Keep it simple and straightforward. Share with them the problems you had because of your addiction problems regarding family relationships, loss of friends, financial and spiritual difficulties and damage to your health. Talk about your attempts to overcome the addiction, your failures, and how you finally came to your present condition.

Don't try to be a hero. You may at some future time become a hero in the person's eyes. But it won't be because you tried to, it will be because they decided to see you in that light. Neither are you a savior or a healer. If someone you try to help recovers, it will be because of a Power greater than yourself. Simply tell your story; let the person know you care and that you are willing to give more help if they desire it. Always remember, you can't make the person well. All you have to offer is your story. If you are going to take credit for the recovery of someone you helped, you will also need to accept the responsibility for those who fail, and that would be a heavy, heavy load.

Remember, too, you are not a banker or an employment security specialist. Do not offer money either as a gift or a loan, because money can burn a hole in any chance they may have for sobriety. Do not offer to find them a job; that is their responsibility. In short, just carry the message, not the body.

We have discussed continuing to take personal inventory, we have discussed prayer and meditation, and we have discussed carrying the message. Combining these into a continuous, on-going daily way of life is what is meant by practicing these principles in all our affairs. That is why I believe it's necessary to become aware and stay aware of our personality defects; to keep them in check; to become aware of our personality assets and keep them in use; to try, through prayer and meditation, to become personally aware of the power and love of God in our lives; and, once having developed this awareness, to use it for the benefit of those with whom we come in contact in our daily living.

Wouldn't it be pleasant to know that when someone says, "I'm glad I met you," they really mean it? That it was not just the habitual, proper thing that we all say when we have met someone new? Wouldn't it be nice to know we have made life a little better for someone just because we are here? Wouldn't it be nice, at the end of the day, to look in a mirror and say, "I like you"?

Finally, be good to yourself; take care of yourself. You are truly a miracle. You are important. Do some happiness.

STEP ONE

We admitted we were powerless over WHATEVER our problem is, that our FEELINGS had become unmanageable.

STEP TWO

Came to believe THAT a power greater than ourselves could restore us to SANITY.

STEP THREE

Made a decision to turn our WANTS and our FEELINGS over to the care of God even though we may not understand Him.

STEP FOUR

Made a searching, SCARY, HONEST inventory of ourselves.

STEP FIVE

Admitted to God, to ourselves and another human being the EXACT nature of our wrongs.

STEP SIX

Were ENTIRELY ready to have God remove ALL these defects of character.

STEP SEVEN

HONESTLY and SINCERELY asked Him to remove our shortcomings.

STEP EIGHT

Made a list of ALL PERSONS we had harmed and became willing to make amends to them ALL.

STEP NINE

Made DIRECT amends to such people wherever possible except when to do so would injure them or others. (Otherwise we made INDIRECT amends.)

STEP TEN

Continued to take a MOMENT-TO-MOMENT personal inventory and when we were wrong PROMPTLY admitted it.

STEP ELEVEN

Sought through prayer and meditation to improve our conscious contact with God even though we may not understand Him, praying, NOT YARPING, only for knowledge of His will for us and the power to carry that out.

STEP TWELVE

Having had a spiritual awakening as a RESULT OF THESE STEPS, we tried to carry this message to alcoholics and to practice these principles in all our affairs.

If you are called upon for help, remember that you are not a hero. Just tell your story. Keep it simple, straightforward, and honest. Live in such a way as to be considered honest and clean, a role model to be respected. In so doing, you will be carrying the message loud and clear.

NOTES

Epilogue

Overheard In An Orchard

Said the Robin to the Sparrow:
"I should really like to know
Why these anxious human beings
Rush about and worry so."

Said the Sparrow to the Robin:
"Friend, I think that it must be
That they have no heavenly Father
Such as cares for you and me."

–Elizabeth Cheney

There is no such thing on this earth as a life without problems. If I have implied otherwise I apologize and stand corrected. From the meanest weed or flower to the giant Sequoia trees, from the tiniest insect to the largest mammal, from a new-born baby to the grave, there are bound to be problems. Sometimes it seems the very elements are lined up against all creation, and life can be hard if we let it be.

But I ask myself what kind of world it would be without adversity. Would we all be living in caves and scratching messages on the walls with a stick? Once on an outing in the Rocky Mountains I saw an evergreen tree growing from a small crack in a granite boulder. The boulder was cracked in such a way that I could see down part way to where the trunk of this little bit of life had struggled to twist and turn its way up and out on its journey to reach the sunlight. Mankind has had to do the same thing in his effort to achieve—what?—a trip to the moon? Or a visit to Mars? An airplane? An automobile? A television set?

They say (I have never figured out who "they" refers to) that necessity is the mother of invention. I personally don't know how necessary it is to go to the moon or to Mars or to the outer reaches of space. I sometimes think "curiosity" is more apt to be the mother of invention. Be that as it may, there are problems involved with the development of our lifestyle and man seems to manage to solve those problems. We have come a long way from writing on the walls of caves.

The point of all this is that we all have problems, have had for centuries, and will continue to have them until the end of time as we know it. But problems aren't trouble. Problems aren't a cause of unhappiness, but trouble usually is. For many years I lived a life of trouble and I was unhappy. Now I know that the trouble was of my own making, that it came from my inability or unwillingness to manage my own character defects. It was said of me, "Vaughn is his own worst enemy." I certainly was, and it was the result of expecting too much and returning too little. To me a problem looked much larger than it was, and I was too often unwilling to apply the necessary effort to overcome. Therefore I let a problem become trouble. I was running my own universe and you know what? I was unqualified to do that.

By the grace of God, through the courage of my son, and with the help of Pepper and many others, I began to apply the Twelve Steps to my way of life and they have become a way of life. It is a good life, a quiet, peaceful life, and through it I have learned to reach out to others, not only to ask for help in solving problems if needed, but to offer help where I can. I am no longer the "master of my fate," but God is, and I am very happy to allow Him to be. He does such a splendid job.

I want to end by returning to my earlier quotation:

"Lord, I ain't what I ought to be,
And Lord, I ain't what I want to be,
And Lord, I ain't what I'm going to be,
But thank you, Lord, I ain't what I used to be."